Losing Your Best Friend

Vacancies of the Heart

By

Frosty Wooldridge

AuthorHouse™
1663 Liberty Drive
Bloomington, IN 47403
www.authorhouse.com
Phone: 1-800-839-8640

© 2010 Frosty Wooldridge. All rights reserved.

No part of this book may be reproduced, stored in a retrieval system, or transmitted by any means without the written permission of the author.

First published by AuthorHouse 1/18/2010

ISBN: 978-1-4490-6222-4 (sc)

Printed in the United States of America
Bloomington, Indiana

This book is printed on acid-free paper.

Dedicated to:

Denis LeMay for a lifetime of shared adventures!

Merci mon ami!

Table of Contents

Foreword viii
Chapter 1—What Makes a Best Friend? 1
Chapter 2—Losing my first best friend 8
Chapter 3—Your father as your best friend 12
Chapter 4—Best friend in high school 17
Chapter 5—First best friend of adult years 22
Chapter 6—How could his wife cost your
    friendship? 29
Chapter 7—Losing friends with changing
    family situation 37
Chapter 8—Power of a friend for growth or
    change of life choices 39
Chapter 9—Best friend as a surrogate father 45
Chapter 10—Spirit friends versus casual friends 50
Chapter 11—Losing a best friend to his best
    friend: booze 57
Chapter 12—Losing a best friend by outside
    factors 63
Chapter 13—Losing a friend via unwanted
    advice 70
Chapter 14—Possible reasons for friendship
    and compatibilities 77
Chapter 15—Dropping a best friend 83
Chapter 16—Losing your brother as a friend 87

Chapter 17—Friends at the later stages of your life 90

Chapter 18—Losing a friend too soon 94

Chapter 19—Do it while you're young 100

Chapter 20—Losing a friend you never met 105

Chapter 21—How to lessen your chances of losing a best friend 109

Epilogue 114

Foreword

As an outdoor-adventure-type male, I consider friendship as one of the foundations of a meaningful life on this planet. Yes, I traveled alone on some of my bicycle adventures around the globe—and still enjoyed myself. I made the adventure my companion, and several times, I met men and women on the same journey who became lifelong friends.

I have gone fishing by myself and backpacked into some remote areas of Colorado and Alaska. At one point, I climbed a 14,000 foot peak alone, but when I reached the top, I found myself talking with myself. Not much fun!

Most of us enjoy solo time like a walk down a country road at sunset to clear our minds. Or, a swim across a lake to refresh our senses! Perhaps we might enjoy a bicycle ride early on a Saturday morning. Still others play solitaire for quiet time. Everybody enjoys a different style.

However, nothing quite brings meaning to an experience like sharing it with a friend. When you spend enough campfires, ski trips, tennis matches, bicycle rides, motorcycle trips, triathlons and fishing expeditions with another like-minded male, you form a 'best friend' relationship that you come to depend on over a lifetime.

It's been said in greeting cards, "A best friend is a miracle of the universe."

I concur. Over my lifetime, a half dozen men arrived at my life's doorstep and walked into my heart. To tell the truth, several women also became my best friends, but with women, they feature different emotional equations. Women create a unique dynamic, don't they?!

Thus, it's never quite the same as a male best friend because women only know how to operate as women. They cannot know how we men function because, well, they possess different perspectives. Their emotions and brains ride a distinctive trolley on a different track.

While they understand each other, we cannot figure them out as verified by 50 percent divorce rates and male-female battles on soap operas.

Wasn't it Freud who asked, "What does a woman want?"

Above all today, America's women create a new equality paradigm for the first time in history. Women often command more money and higher status. They drive nicer cars. Many give men orders. Women work jobs formerly commandeered by men such as firefighters, jet fighter pilots, soldiers, military generals, law officers, park rangers, CEOs, front loader operators and police chiefs.

Therefore, men band together to find a sense of masculine camaraderie they cannot find with the fairer sex.

But in the process of women's new found power in America and many western societies, different paradigms surfaced. Women took command in marriages by becoming the dominant partner. This created new challenges for men as you will discover in these pages.

Therefore, male friendships in the 21st century find themselves in jeopardy. Best friendships, built on years of shared experiences, crack and dismantle at the hands of forces outside their ability to maintain themselves.

On the balance sheet, however, over the years, I watched men dominate their women or wives to such an extent that they wouldn't allow them to enjoy girlfriends or other male friends on a platonic level. Thus the 'friendship' drama cannot be considered one-sided. Inequities ride with both sexes.

I did, however, attempt to interview over a dozen women for their stories, but found scant responses. Therefore, I hope a female author, at some point, tackles the 'friendship' issue from the feminine side in the future.

Beyond that, in these pages, you will meet my friends as well as others who shared their stories about their best friends. You will discover how those men lost their friends and how I lost mine. You may rediscover some of your own best friends. You may find your stomach stirring as you remember long-ago friendships in your life.

You might remember all the good times, the parties, the women, the beers, the dancing and the campfires that created that 'best friend' with whom you shared your greatest stories. You also shared your hopes and sorrows. You may find that your best friends gave you greater wisdom, taught you lessons and brought greater dimension to your life.

But when they vanished from your sphere, for whatever reason, it left a hole in your heart. They became missing pieces from the grand mural of your life. While you built those deep bonds with them over the years, you never anticipated their being ripped out of your life, or dying or leaving on their own.

Additionally, you may have exited a friendship. Why? Let's explore that together.

These pages constitute a tribute to all those best friends in my life. They brought me hilarity and a sense of well-being. They shared some pretty good laughs along the way. They created that laughter and they made the best of our time together.

Along the journey, I brought great moments to their lives and a uniquely compelling sense of friendship that lasts for ages in their minds.

At the same time, this book fills a few vacancies of the heart. I drilled into several areas that brought buckets of tears. What part of losing my best friends did I play? What changes might I have made to ensure the friendship continued? Do some friendships die from distance? Do they die from losing similar interests?

Do our wives or girlfriends possess the power to kill our best friendships? Do politics and religion play a part in friendships? You'll find out in this book. And perhaps, you might discover how to change course for a better outcome.

Finally, it would prove most interesting to see 'why' these losses occurred from the perspective of the guys or even their women. Life takes two to tango, and in the dance, everyone brings a different interpretation.

In only telling my side of the story, which may not be enough, it may be your story, too.

For the friends now gone from my life, I suffer pains in my mind, but celebrate their walking into my heart to make life a great adventure. To each of them, I salute their journey and thank them for those campfires and the laughter, and for each one of them at one time for becoming my best friend.

Frosty Wooldridge
Louisville, CO

Chapter 1—
What Makes a Best Friend?

"A best friend will always tell you his or her take about situations which confront you, regardless of your positions. Such a friend will often do something for you unasked and expect no reciprocity. If you are ill or in need of any kind of assistance, such a friend will at least offer to help—while maybe not able, for example, to make a large financial advance—but can make you aware that there is real commitment to be as helpful as possible—not just saying, "Is there anything I can do?" which is a frequent way of doing nothing."
                                                        Don Collins

Without a doubt, a mysterious chemistry creates best friendships. I have watched some of the finest men bond with other dudes that seemed totally at odds. At other times, I have seen alpha males bond with other dominant males via sports, but their competitive personalities led to caustic outcomes.

Once in awhile, two highly competitive males may bond because their personalities don't collide via their egos. At other times, two non-dominant males become best friends because neither threatens the other.

Sometimes, a high powered male befriends a lesser male to boost his own sense of maleness.

Several of my best friends matched my athletic skills, which created excellent bonding that led to long term friendships. There's nothing quite like sharing physical, raw adventure. It may be the purest form of friendship whereby you share great moments, scary moments, dangerous moments or triumph at the top of a 14er or rafting class fives or other adrenalin producing activities. Sheer exhilaration creates an amazing bond between men.

On a mental level, several literary friends matched my passion for writing, but couldn't accompany me on highly physical ventures like backpacking, mountain climbing or bike racing. That kind of a male bonding remained in the intellectual realm.

One of my best friends became my spiritual 'best friend' whereby we bonded at church, but beyond the sanctuary, we lived separate lives.

Some guys make friends with another man because he may serve as a father figure. How does that happen? The first guy makes friends with an older man or near the same age because the first guy lost his father or his father drank himself to death or a dozen other reasons. Not having a father creates a need to find someone that recognizes 'you' live and breathe.

While you may enjoy 'acquaintances' at work or play or church or civic groups, that 'best friend' chemistry remains a mystery right up there with the "Big Bang Theory" or "What do women want?"

But once you make that stunning connection, everything feels 'right' with the world. You can call your best friend to figure out a problem, hit the road on your motorcycles, spend a day on the slopes, share a fishing trip, or hunt or climb any mountain. It's been said that 'best friends' share one spirit in two bodies.

My friend Don said, "Having a best friend is a wonderful, exhilarating and rarely achieved state for many people at any age. Never letting too much time pass without realizing, considering and celebrating your good fortune with such a person is a cardinal rule for me. I feel fortunate to thus have a number of "best friends" all of whom I celebrate and savor. Maintaining friendships has something to do with one's energy and mental acuity, but mostly with that rare and precious commodity—time."

"Does this mean I am unwilling to make a "best friend" commitment?" you ask.

Not at all! But "best friend for what" might be a better definition. My golfing friends, for example, are "best friends" for that department, but might not ever want to discuss other matters which are an integral part of my whole self. There are others who want to discuss politics, even religion, or perhaps art and music, whose company I crave.

A longtime friend Herb said, "One of my other best friends was one that never criticized me. He took long walks with me and listened to me. Sometimes he interrupted me and wanted to cuddle in my lap. That was my dog, Boo. Great friend! It was sad when we buried Boo many years ago. But I have fond memories of my best friend, Boo."

Herb added, "My friends are the ones that agree with me. They are the ones that disagree with me, and tell me why. My friends are those that I have shared experiences with. Shared ideas with! Shared good times and bad times! My daughter once told me, "Dad, sometimes you act like an ass when you meet new people. Next time when you meet someone, welcome them into your life as your new best friend." Thank you daughter Karyn! You are one of my best friends for telling me that."

Who, in the end, must be your best friend, day in and day out? Herb said, "Right now, I am one of my best friends. I plan on going out and enjoying this day with Herb and see who else is out there to celebrate today with. Maybe I will meet a new best friend."

My long time German friend Gerd said, "My former best friend turned 50 earlier this year and when I went to his party I felt I didn't belong anymore. His life has been always in my little town of less than 1,000 inhabitants and I have been around the world, got to know new and different people from different cultures, backgrounds and races. Now I felt we were just talking about our youth but otherwise we didn't have anything to talk about. I felt lost and knew I didn't belong anymore.

"Well, life happens but I have found so many new friends over the years who have not always kept in touch. I am not sad or mad about this fact. It happens! People evolve and friendships come and go even so this was a special one, and when we were between 12 and 20, we did everything together. It was great. It is a bit sad but like I said before, people evolve and obviously it happens they often evolve in different directions.

"A big point I think is when one of the guys gets married and the other doesn't. The wife looks upon THE friend sometimes like a competitor and tries to loosen the ties. It actually happened with my long time girlfriend who wanted to claim me all for herself and I saw friendships slipping away."

I have more to say about Gerd's experience in another chapter.

My Venezuelan friend Juan said, "When I left Venezuela to study in the USA, I left my neighboring friends and playmates of cowboys and Indians when I was nine years old. We shared that "chemical togetherness" of being one more brother with whom one shares the adventure or creativity of imagination of a different place in a different time era. Most of our characters were taken from comic books of the time, Roy Rogers, Red Ryder, Hopalong Cassidy, the Lone Ranger and of course Buck Rogers. It was the sharing of creativity in adding features that were not in the comic books themselves, but in our imagination that we gleefully enjoyed among ourselves.

"The first experience of making new friends in a foreign country is to find common adventure ground.

"The joy of climbing a chestnut tree to its full height, regardless of the initial language barrier, made communication much easier in action, not so much in words. "Gee whiz, he does the same as we do and enjoys it" would probably be their exclamation. It was the joy of being together and doing things that we all liked. This togetherness made up for the absence of being far away from home and from being absent from mom and dad. It taught you to be creative and to shield oneself from your own weaker feelings of loneliness. This feeling of being alone was the main factor of being united, regardless of where we came from."

COSMIC FRIENDS

My Australian friend John, with whom I bicycled across America coast to coast, said, "I like your quote about a best friend is a miracle of the universe."

"When you extend friendship into the universal 'friendshop', new limits operate," John said. "Just look into the night sky. They are the friends of the lonely sailor. They are the friends of those who wander the deserts.

"They are the stars that have kept humanity company for millennia. Something as universal as stars endures beyond friendship in this mortality. You are born under the stars and leave the same way. Some say you come back again to give it another go and the memory of the stars is reacquainted.

"This is the stuff that warms the spirit. Bonds of such friendship have a cosmic feel. Now if one is lucky enough to have a cosmic friend then there is a friend for life, even lifetimes.

"I know of such friends that endure beyond normal dimensionality. Do you ever get a pull toward such a jewel of nature? Ever felt part of you is up there in the stars? Maybe like a part of your higher nature? Imagine if you had a higher nature and found it. What sort of friendship would that be? What bond could be stronger than finding your lost half? No reunion could be more immense. What longing is more binding than such a coming together?

"It is the concept that is within as well as without that deepens ones individuality."

Whatever the heck creates such a friendship, life feels better and the sun shines brighter.

Chapter 2—
Losing my first best friend

"Sometimes, you never realize how much better your life is with your best friend until you lose him for some reason."
                                        Jason Rogers

As a military brat, I moved with my parents every two to three years from base to base and one part of the world to another. By the time I reached 12 candles on my cake, my homes included Chicago, Illinois, Cadillac, Michigan, Quantico, Virginia, Paris Island, South Carolina and Kaneohe, Oahu, Hawaii.

We lived 30 yards from the surf in a beach cabana. White sands, blue waters, crashing waves, palm trees and a small island 50 yards off shore became my world. We ran bare foot to school in T-shirts every day of the year. I can't imagine a more idyllic childhood.

Next door, I made friends with Danny Newberry. Skinny kid with a mop of brown hair and freckles just like me! We climbed coconut trees, swam in the surf and waded out to the island at low tide. You couldn't imagine a better "Tom Sawyer and Huckleberry Finn" friendship.

We sat in the same class at school trying to out-study and out-grade each other in the academic area

Losing Your Best Friend

while we battled on the soccer field to beat each other. We played on the same baseball team as both our dads coached us. Hits, runs, double plays, pitching and catching brought us dramatic athletic ups and downs, wins and losses.

Yeah, we talked with girls once in awhile, but they seemed like beings from another planet. They didn't enter into our lives other than irritations when they tried to gain our attention.

In the summer, which was all year, we grabbed our flippers, goggles and snorkels for sojourns out to the island. Magic occurs when you're a kid on a grand adventure to an island full of mysteries much like Captain Jack Sparrow, Robinson Crusoe or "Castaway" with Tom Hanks. We swam, waded and made our way through crystal waters filled with tiny fish, sea stars, urchins and all sorts of crabs. On the island itself, rare birds squawked at us while we climbed coconut trees and grabbed the prize. We cut them open, punched holes into them and sucked out the coconut milk nectar. We broke open the shells to eat the white meat.

One day, on our way out to the island, we watched a large ray gliding around in a reef pool beneath us. That mesmerizing creature of uncommon beauty captured our attention while we floated on the surface, spit water out of our snorkels and witnessed another miracle of nature. I bet Danny still recounts that day to his family members and I know for a fact, that he still utters my name, too.

How do I know? Simple! I talk about him to all my friends.

What factor created our bond? Time together and adventures! As you heard from Juan's description earlier, friendships grow via mutual time and exploits. We shared amazing moments for real--just like Tom and Huck.

I loved Danny even though he outran me and beat me in soccer games. I never thought about how he felt, but as a kid, I lived and played my life and since he shared in it, we grew into a 'best friendship' that suited us while it nurtured us.

As a kid, however, you never think about friendship. You participate while not being aware of the gift. You go about your business with the blessings of friendship, but never appreciate it or the miracle of it.

Then, one day, my dad sat us down at the dinner table, "Well, I just got transferred to Camp Lejeune, North Carolina. We'll be leaving in 30 days. We'll still be near the beach so you won't skip a beat."

Military personnel don't have a choice as to duty assignment. We might not skip a beat regarding the beach, but my friend Danny would be 6,000 miles away.

Thirty days passed faster than a wave crashes on a beach in Hawaii.

"Danny, I'll write you," I said on our last day together.

"I'll write you, too," he said. "Hey, we're friends for life!"

As a kid, tears somehow don't explain your pain nor do they solve the problem. I never saw Danny again. I don't know how much he hurt after we parted, but it's been most of my lifetime that I've missed my first best friend with no chance to reconnect. No chance to talk about our adventures on the island, no chance to share more good times, and no chance to continue our friendship. When you tear away from the emotional moorings of a friend, your lifelines fray more than you realize.

For whatever reason, we wrote a few letters, but then the river of life carried us into new realms of our lives.

Still, he's my best friend for life just like Tom Sawyer and Huck Finn!

Chapter 3—
Your father as your best friend

"My dad meant the world to me. I'll never have a best friend as nice as my dad. He taught me how to live life. He never said he loved me; he didn't have to. He expressed it every day of my youth."

Richard Hollings

Let's face it, our fathers guide us, take us in hand and lead us into life via adventures, everyday living and role modeling. Their actions speak louder than their words. Some dads do a good job while others do a terrible job.

My father remains my best friend over 40 years since his passing. He helped me through many traumatic moments in my young life, or at least to me, those challenges seemed horrendous at the time. Among his many gifts on my way to manhood, he always put his hand on my shoulder with the words, "Son, you can do that."

My dad instilled in me the powerful intention that whatever the challenge, "I can do it!" No matter how many failures I've experienced in my life, I carry the indelible ink on my brain that success remains within my grasp as a man.

For example, during my 10th grade year, I saw a picture of the Wall of China in a world history book. I told my teacher, Mrs. Rainwater, that I would one day walk on the Wall of China. She said, "You can't ever do that; the country of China is closed to all foreigners."

I responded, "My dad said things always change so one day, I will walk on the Wall of China!"

And in November of 1984, I walked on the Wall of China.

When I graduated from college, I promised myself to ride my bicycle across seven continents. With my dad's incredible gift, I've ridden six continents with the seventh one well in sight.

For several years, I have competed in the toughest mountain bike race in the world: "Leadville 100 Mountain Bike Race Across the Sky." It includes starting at 10,152 feet. From there riders must ride over four 12,000 foot passes and one 13,000 foot pass. They must complete it in 12 hours to gain a silver buckle. In one day, they must pedal up 16,000 vertical feet of rocky, dangerous, one track mountain trails. To say the least, it's a deadly, God forsaken physical nightmare. I've ridden it four times and never earned the silver buckle.

However, on August 9, 2008, I stood on the starting line to compete against Lance Armstrong, the seven time world champion of the Tour de France. For the first five seconds, I raced neck and neck with him. Then, only his dust in my eyes!

Nonetheless, I raced over the first two 12,000 foot passes and pedaled my way up the 13,000 footer when Armstrong and David Wiens, who had already conquered the 13,000 footer—raced right at me.

"Here comes Lance," I muttered as I gasped for air.

As they raced toward me, I jumped off and stood astride my bike, "I salute you gentlemen!"

They saluted me back!

For me, that silver buckle came in a distant second to my great moment racing against Lance Armstrong in the toughest bicycle race in the world.

Thanks Dad for giving me the guts, gumption and grit when you said, "Son, you can do that!"

Don said, "I finally understood that my father was my best friend only after we were both well along in years. It was not because he hadn't been that all along, but that I was too immature to realize that he and my mother had given so much to make me strong and independent. Dad was basically quite shy, had a rather stern demeanor, but was deeply committed to his family and honest to the core.

"If it takes a village to raise a child, which I believe is the case; they were the senior officials of my small jurisdiction. In my generation's upbringing years, the 1930s and 1940s, parental roles were much more defined than now. The father's function was to bring discipline, practical advice on the world and encouraging direction to sons, who frankly, were subject to more attention than daughters. Mine certainly filled that role and helped in every way to guide my errant steps from teen to middle life, when suddenly our relationship became one of peer to peer, which meant a warm flowering of emotions and exchanges I shall always treasure.

"At the end of his life, when his terminal cancer burst full force, I sat at his bedside for two months and tried to pay back the enormous debt of caring and love which he had given me."

Juan relates a beautiful memory of his dad, "My late father was my best friend because I could talk to him openly and confide in him on my worries about life and my surroundings, mainly because he always told me the truth and never lied to me as other relatives did. As a young kid I would sit with him on the front porch of our house after dinner and "tell him stories" instead of the usual other way around when normally it's our parents who tell us stories. He would listen with amusement at my imagination and asked me where I got such ideas and so on.

"It was in this story telling to him that I got accustomed to trust him and ask him whatever I was getting curious about. The most crucial time of my life was when I was reaching my puberty or beginning my adolescent life that I asked him about women in general. He explained to me in very sincere way about the facts of life without any metaphors, much less no BS. He was frank and realistic.

"The main characteristic about any friendship is sincerity as well as honesty. These two factors lead up to respect and solidarity which is a pedestal that rests on the foundation of the previous two factors. From then on, the column goes upward with many other virtues, like love, admiration, brotherhood and a fraternal support in all types of situations.

"I had to mention my father-son relationship before going forward in this paragraph, so that you, dear reader, would understand an honest and sincere relationship based on sincerity and a willingness to help another human being, whether it be your son, a brother, a school buddy, or whatever. It is the willingness to be helpful, demonstrating a very simple mandate that we find in the Holy Bible: *"Love thy fellow man as thou loves oneself."*

"Many people have doubts or confusions about "loving somebody" because it is mistakenly interpreted as a sexual love, which is desire. Loving somebody does not necessarily have to include sex in it, since one loves mom, dad, sister or a friend but it is a different type of love that encloses fraternal bond, admiration and solidarity to stand up for that person no matter what. Ask yourself how many people do you know that fit that description. Don't be afraid to say that you love someone of the same sex or somebody else, thinking that you might be embarrassed or do harm to the other person.

"You simply let him-her know that you admire that person and let that person know that you are his or her friend. I know of people that are afraid to manifest themselves since they are afraid of having their feelings hurt. That is normal and it's a defensive position. After my first boarding school experience, I learned "defensively" to contain myself with my human emotions."

Chapter 4—
Best friend in high school

"Hey dude, I'm Giesie and I'm easy! Let's go skiing and see what those bumps on Sterling Way look like. It's a good day for a good time!"
                                        Mike Giesie

Billy Cannon stood 6'6" tall, spoke with a deep-throated southern drawl and everybody liked him. He never said an unkind word to anyone under the sun. In the 10th grade, he drove a beat-up Ford jalopy without his driver's license.

I entered Dougherty High School, Albany, Georgia that fall. As the new kid on the block, several guys needed to test me in the male pecking order. In class one morning, one of the high school punks, named Bobby Backus stabbed me in the butt with a pen as I walked back from the drinking fountain. I instinctively grabbed his hand, "Don't ever do that again or I'll slap you cross-eyed."

He yelled, "I'll meet you in the park to whup your ass after school. Be there or I'm coming after you."

At that moment, Ms. Clyatt walked into the room to 'quiet' the exchange.

Every time my dad changed duty stations, the local toughs tested my brother and me by taunting, slaps and pimp jobs. If we didn't respond, they continued their various forms of torture. If we expected to live through our high school days in peace, we must stand our ground.

Our dad said, "Fighting is not the answer, but if all else fails, you need to defend yourself. The other guy may get a meal out of you, but if you take a bite out of him, he won't bother you anymore."

Later in the day, Billy walked up to me in the hall, "Heard you're gonna' fight Backus in the park after school. Billy referred to Tullamassy Park near the campus.

"Yeah, he stabbed me in the rear-end this morning," I said. "So I kinda' slapped him up-side the head."

"You're talking some rough characters with Bobby," Billy said. "I better go with you to see that they all don't pile on you."

"Thanks, Billy," I said.

That afternoon, with four of his buddies backing him up, and Billy standing by me, Backus and I pounded on each other. Unfortunately, for Backus, I proved quicker with my punches. Because I played football and didn't smoke, I maintained myself while he gasped for breath. Within five minutes, I locked him down on the ground and administered two black eyes.

All four of his buddies moved toward me.

"Ah, you boys keep your distance!" Billy warned.

They backed off.

Losing Your Best Friend

After the fight, Billy made certain the other dudes didn't pile on top of me.

From there on out, Billy and I remained best friends all through high school. We played on the basketball team that won the Class AAA state title. Of all my athletic pictures from high school, I treasure the one with Billy and me palming basketballs in both our hands.

Unfortunately, after high school, I never saw him again.

I learned a painful lesson in the ensuing years. Some friends continue as friends only as long as you remain in day-to-day contact from a job or mutual sports activities. Some men maintain contact after they bond with you, while others don't. If you're the one more emotionally attached, you will discover great disappointment as the other guy goes about his life and leaves you in his memories with no regrets.

Juan said, "The saddest loss of a friend is the one that you do not expect to be gone from this world. It has happened to me with a childhood friend in my adult years. Strange enough, we last saw each other at a hardware store, on the same road where he was killed in a traffic accident by a speeder. He was more than a friend; he was another brother with whom I shared the innocence and illusions of a child as we grew up in our own fantasy world of games in our backyards, separated only by a chicken wire fence. We shared each other's joys and stories of school classes, mocking our teachers for being so strict, yet so Victorian in their proceedings. I cried when I went to the funeral home to say my last goodbye to him and tried to console his son upon the loss of his father. I was tongue tied aside from not being able to find adequate words to say to a 12 year old boy. I knew that from heaven above he was watching and that he had the consolation of seeing protection to those left behind by the friends here on earth that he had made."

Brian A. Chalker wrote a compelling poem as to the different kinds of friendships—"Reason, Season, Lifetime":

Chalker said, "People always come into your life for a reason, a season or a lifetime. When you figure out which it is, you know exactly what to do. When someone is in your life for a reason, it is usually to meet a need you have expressed outwardly or inwardly. They have come to assist you through a difficulty, or to provide you with guidance and support, to aid you physically, emotionally, or even spiritually. Then, without any wrong doing on your part or at an inconvenient time, this person will say or do something to bring the relationship to an end."

I have found Chalker's words right on the money. As painful as it is, he understands human demeanor. A friendship may come to an end and you cannot do anything to change it.

Chalker wrote about items beyond your control, "Sometimes they die; sometimes they just walk away. Sometimes they act up or out and force you to take a stand. What we must realize is that our need has been met, our desire fulfilled; their work is done. The prayer you sent up has been answered and it is now time to move on."

Chalker added that people come into our lives for a season. When that happens, you benefit for the number of days or years they grace your life and you grace theirs. He relates how they bring you peace and help you laugh. They might even teach you something. For the most part, friends bring you joy!

Other friends come into your life for your entire existence. They give you solid spiritual and emotional foundation.

While Brian Chalker writes eloquently about three kinds of friendship, other factors make for painful realities for many of us who thought 'that' best friend of ours would remain in our lives for a lifetime rather than a season. As we shall find out, many times, we don't enjoy a choice because of outside factors.

Chapter 5—
First best friend of adult years

"Friendship comes from complete trust of your emotions into the hands of another person."
Jon Henderson

High school slipped into my rearview mirrors faster than a red light turns to green! I never saw any of my classmates at Dougherty High School, Albany, Georgia until the 10th reunion. More on that later!

I drove 1,000 miles away to college. That first night at Michigan State University, I sat in the window of 433 North Wonders with tears pouring down my cheeks.

"Man, you are too far away from home," I muttered to myself. "What have you gotten yourself into?"

Freshman year presented many challenges with a gathering war in Vietnam, the draft and being all by myself on a 40,000 student campus. Dorm administrators stuck me with two guys who proved totally incompatible. But soon, I gravitated to the racquetball court and weight room.

Losing Your Best Friend

I met a guy named Ed who taught me how to play racquetball. We played every day, and he beat the snot out of me. I didn't mind because our friendship grew. I liked Ed's confidence, in fact, his arrogance at his athletic talents. We ate dinner together, checked out the chicks coming into the dining room and talked about sports.

But soon, my quickness and speed caught up with Ed on the racquetball court. I beat him one out of five games; soon, two out of five; then, three out of five; then, four out of five; and finally, I beat him five out of five—regularly. He got pissed more than could be called normal. He tried every tactic to beat me. He tried to serve and play faster, but I maintained top shape. He tried different techniques. Didn't help him!

Off the court, he made fun of me, chided me and, after awhile, he berated me.

Yet, we played racquetball with a vengeance! Too many times, he hit me with the ball on purpose, which feels like getting shot and leaves a tennis ball-sized welt on the skin. He ran into me a few times and once, slammed me to the floor.

"That's not a part of the game, Ed!" I retorted. "Don't run into me again like that or find a new partner."

"Can't take the game?" Ed yelled.

"Ed, you're angry because you can't beat me anymore," I said.

"Serve it up buddy! I'll kick your ass!" he yelled.

"No, in fact, I'm too fast for you," I said. "You'll never beat me again in your whole life."

THAT proved a fatal comment. It enraged him!

We never spoke again. He ignored me. I ignored him.

Life moved forward for both of us.

During spring quarter, I met a guy named Phil in the weight room who offered to share his room because the U.S. Army drafted his roommate. After two quarters with my two roommates in a dorm room meant for two guys, I jumped all over that one.

Since Phil only lifted weights and worked out in gymnastics, we didn't compete against each other except that he out bench pressed me. I didn't care if he could bench 425 and I could only push 375. I just wanted to get along.

By the end of spring term, we became fast friends. We signed up for the same room in the fall.

That summer, I worked for United Air Lines as a baggage handler. I made friends with a fellow MSU student named Bob. We shared a great summer together, but he wasn't the athletic type and drank a lot.

Amazingly, because of the Internet and a letter to the editor I wrote that he read in Winter Park, Colorado where he retired 40 years later, we re-connected. He's a great guy and bicycled from the Arctic Circle, Norway to Athens, Greece with me.

In the fall of that school year, Phil and I moved into our dorm room. Living with a dude whom you like and who shares your values and athletic pursuits proved a match made in heaven. We got along like two peas in a pod. Never a cross word!

We chased coeds at the dances, talked about his gymnastics, about getting stronger with weights, classes and the war.

He became my best friend. Fall term flew past. In Michigan in the autumn, the trees turn every color of the rainbow. Crisp air greets college kids in the morning with blue skies and geese flying over campus all day. Thousands landed in the fields south of campus to put on an aerial show that astounded viewers.

Winter term arrived. Phil and I remained inseparable. He helped me with math courses and I helped him with English classes. I taught him a few jitterbug moves that had women lining up to dance with him at the Sunday night 'mixers'.

After that, women lined up to dance with us more than we could handle. He showed me how to change my grip for the bench press to gain more leverage. We took a kinesiology class together and studied our butts off. We each earned an 'A' from the class!

Spring term swept onto campus with lightning speed. Our friendship made every day a good day. After having lost my dad, I enjoyed Phil as a man whom I trusted and shared sports.

That next fall quarter, we signed up for the same room. Everything worked out until Phil walked into the room one morning with a gray, ashen face.

"Well dude," he said. "The U.S. Army has my ass in a sling."

"What?" I said. "What happened to your 2-S deferment?"

"My grades weren't high enough," Phil said. "I have to report to Fort Benning, Georgia for basic training."

By that time, 300 U.S. soldiers lost their lives every week in Vietnam. Students protested in the streets. At the 1968 Democratic Convention in Chicago, they rioted. At Kent State, National Guard troops shot several students dead on campus. Everybody hated President Johnson and after him, Nixon.

I sickened at the prospect of Phil's going to Vietnam. Letters to the editor by former MSU students exposed the war as a death trap perpetrated by politicians.

"We're dying for nothing over here," one soldier ranted.

Each day the State News reported another MSU student suffered death or wounds from fighting the Vietcong. We watched Napalm burn up entire villages. Lt. Calley and Captain Medina oversaw the My Lai Massacre whereby soldiers killed an entire village of civilians. Most of the letters to the editor expressed outrage at the U.S. government forcing young men into jungles where you never knew where the enemy hid. Snipers picked men off like shooting ducks in a pond. Drafted troops fragged their commanding officers in the field, killing some of them. The war drove many to madness, anger and killing.

Little known about Vietnam, 150,000 to as high as 200,000 troops that served over there, committed suicide years after the war from their psychological trauma.

Losing Your Best Friend

Today, it's called 'Post Traumatic Stress Syndrome'. To give you an idea of the horror of war, with 58,300 dead from battle wounds, upwards of 200,000 died of emotional wounds. Tens of thousands more died from cancer from such chemicals used over in Nam known as Agent Orange. My brother-in-law, U.S. Navy, Ken McKinney suffered death 20 years later via Agent Orange, which he loaded every day while aboard ship. It lodged in his pancreas. He died of pancreatic cancer at 48 leaving my sister and their two kids.

After advanced infantry training at Fort Polk, Louisiana, Phil received his orders for Vietnam.

He came to visit me before he shipped out.

We talked about his experiences.

"I'm scared Frosty," he said as a matter of fact. "Good chance of dying over there!"

While the shock of Phil's being drafted out of our dorm room hadn't worn off, my new roommate proved a basket case of insecurities and girl problems.

Mort threw fits of anger, felt like his penis needed to be larger and wanted to marry a gal who wanted to become a nun. He drove me nuts.

Months later, Phil made one last visit.

"I don't know what to say Phil," I said. "I could be next."

Before he turned to leave the room, he pulled a gold peace ring out of his pocket.

"Here, wear this," he said. "If I come back from Nam, I'll take you out for a beer and tell you stories. If I don't come back, wear this ring and become a man of peace for the rest of your life."

About every two weeks, I received a detailed letter from Phil describing the insanity of what happened daily in Vietnam. His letters became my history book on brutal occurrences in the war zone. I cried over each letter.

Three months later, Phil died in a firefight in something known as the Tet Offensive.

I ached deeper in my gut than anyone understood. My father's loss left me with an empty emotional 'gut shot' that took years to heal. Now, three years later, my best friend died senselessly and brutally. I walked around in a second daze at the loss of someone dear to me. Back then, we didn't enjoy grief counseling or any other kind of help. I just wandered through my days with a gut ache, mind ache and depressed spirit.

By that time, we knew the war proved a fraud. Secretary Robert McNamara, years later, wrote in his book that Vietnam was a mistake. He promoted the war based on the "Domino Theory" that we must stop communism before it took over the world. Instead, we didn't try to win the war, but kept getting shot and losing young men until 1975. In the end, 58,300 deaths and 350,000 horribly wounded!

When I visit Washington, DC, I walk to the Vietnam Memorial Wall. I become sad, depressed and melancholy. I walk over to Phil's name engraved in the black granite stone. I run my hands over his name etched for eternity. Always, I am reduced to sobbing, endless tears and sadness more profound than most can imagine. But then, 58,300 other family members also cry in their own pain.

Over 40 years later, I still miss my best friend Phil.

Chapter 6—
How could his wife cost your friendship?

"The values that make a best friend are quite a few, since it is a bond that involves a close relationship of confidence and trust. It is the person that you can count on in good times and bad, regardless if it's a man or a woman. It also involves a mutual respect, admiration and shielding attitude in keeping that friend out of harm's way and wishing the best for him or her and his family. People are good friends because they see things likewise."
Juan Herrera

At our commencement, my whole floor cheered as we threw our caps into the air. Graduation from college marks a milestone in a man's life. It's a stepping off place into adult life. You're no longer a kid. You can't go home. You don't get two weeks off at Christmas, one week at spring break and three months in the summer.

All of a sudden, you need a job. You must buy a car, rent an apartment, pay for food, insurance, electricity and water. You must wash your own laundry and clean your apartment.

In my last two years of college, I made three more friends in Jesse, Bobby and Steve. We grew pretty tight. We skied, biked, backpacked, camped, played tennis and canoed together. We chased women at the parties.

However, Jesse took a teaching job in Lake Tahoe, Nevada. Since we all three acquired teaching jobs, summers proved a blast.

Jesse invited me out to his wedding. I decided to ride my motorcycle from Denver to Lake Tahoe. You know, into the wind, freedom, Easy Rider and all that wild man stuff!

When I rolled into town, I grabbed Jesse in a bear hug. We laughed, joked and stepped out for pizza and beer. Just like old times in college! He told jokes while I laughed my head off. Can't beat it!

At the wedding, his smiling bride, Melinda, seemed to grit her teeth at me in a way I couldn't understand. In the reception line, she winced when I gave her a hug. However, I gave a glowing toast to the bride and groom that melted every heart in the joint.

Nonetheless, like a guy playing golf on a sunny day, I wasn't ready for a lightning strike out of a blue sky.

The next day, as I packed up my gear, Jesse accompanied me to my motorcycle.

"Hey man, great to have you come to the wedding," he said. "I got a few things I have to talk to you about."

In the course of 15 minutes, he told me how our values differed since college and that our friendship couldn't continue. I stood by my bike dumbfounded. Then, I threw a leg over my motorcycle still dazed

Losing Your Best Friend

at what he said. In effect, he said our friendship had ended.

"Jesse," I said, "I don't know what to say, but I wish you the best in your marriage and life. Thanks for your honesty and all the good times in college. You're a hell of a friend and a hell of a man!"

I fired up the bike, dropped the clutch, gave a good-bye wave and never saw him again. I did notice his wife in the window as I drove off.

A year later, my old buddy Bobby invited me to his wedding. All the old floor mates attended. During the Catholic Mass, we sat bored to tears as we knew his gal, Julie resembled the woman played by Kathleen Turner married to Michael Douglas in the movie, "War of Roses."

When the priest announced them man and wife, he said, "Not only do Bob and Julie walk down the aisle today, but they walk with Jesus."

Golbeski, one of the floor's funny guys, said, "Three's a crowd; kick out Jesus!"

A pall of silence rippled through the church crowd. It reminded me of the poem by Ernest Thayer "Casey at the Bat":

The Outlook wasn't brilliant for the Mudville nine that day: The score stood four to two, with but one inning more to play. And then when Cooney died at first, and Barrows did the same, A sickly silence fell upon the patrons of the game.

A straggling few got up to go in deep despair. The rest Clung to that hope which springs eternal in the human breast; They thought, if only Casey could get but a whack at that - We'd put up even money, now, with Casey at the bat.

But Flynn preceded Casey, as did also Jimmy Blake, And the former was a lulu and the latter was a cake; So upon that stricken multitude grim melancholy sat, For there seemed but little chance of Casey's getting to the bat.

But Flynn let drive a single, to the wonderment of all, And Blake, the much despised, tore the cover off the ball; And when the dust had lifted, and the men saw what had occurred, There was Jimmy safe at second and Flynn a-hugging third.

Then from 5,000 throats and more there rose a lusty yell; It rumbled through the valley, it rattled in the dell; It knocked upon the mountain and recoiled upon the flat, For Casey, mighty Casey, was advancing to the bat.

There was ease in Casey's manner as he stepped into his place; There was pride in Casey's bearing and a smile on Casey's face. And when, responding to the cheers, he lightly doffed his hat, No stranger in the crowd could doubt 'twas Casey at the bat.

Ten thousand eyes were on him as he rubbed his hands with dirt; Five thousand tongues applauded when he wiped them on his shirt. Then while the writhing pitcher ground the ball into his hip, Defiance gleamed in Casey's eye, a sneer curled Casey's lip.

And now the leather-covered sphere came hurtling through the air, And Casey stood a-watching it in haughty grandeur there. Close by the sturdy batsman the ball unheeded sped- "That ain't my style," said Casey. "Strike one," the umpire said.

Losing Your Best Friend

From the benches, black with people, there went up a muffled roar, Like the beating of the storm-waves on a stern and distant shore. "Kill him! Kill the umpire!" shouted someone on the stand; And its likely they'd a-killed him had not Casey raised his hand.

With a smile of Christian charity great Casey's visage shone; He stilled the rising tumult; he bade the game go on; He signaled to the pitcher, and once more the spheroid flew; But Casey still ignored it, and the umpire said, "Strike two."

"Fraud!" cried the maddened thousands, and echo answered fraud; But one scornful look from Casey and the audience was awed. They saw his face grow stern and cold, they saw his muscles strain, And they knew that Casey wouldn't let that ball go by again.

The sneer is gone from Casey's lip, his teeth are clenched in hate; He pounds with cruel violence his bat upon the plate. And now the pitcher holds the ball, and now he lets it go, And now the air is shattered by the force of Casey's blow.

Oh, somewhere in this favored land the sun is shining bright; The band is playing somewhere, and somewhere hearts are light, And somewhere men are laughing, and somewhere children shout; But there is no joy in Mudville - mighty Casey has struck out.

Everybody knew Bobby's life as he knew it would not last another day. But the game would go on!

For kicks and grins, at the reception, around 11:00 p.m., when the dance floor filled and everybody walked a little tipsy, one of Bob's buddies backed his bike up to the front reception door and revved the engine. His Harley blasted smoke and noise into the reception like what you see at the legendary Sturgis, South Dakota motorcycle rally.

Everybody cheered but Julie's mother. Bobby's mom raced toward his friend with the look of Nurse Ratchet from "One Flew Over the Cuckoo's Nest" with Jack Nicholson.

Bobby, who loved riding motorcycles, sold his bike within a month of marrying Julie.

"I've outgrown motorcycles," he told me.

Then he gave me the same speech Jesse gave me. In fact, he gave every guy on the floor the same speech.

Years later, Bobby, armed with a Ph.D., became the head of the Economics Department at a major university. He filed for divorce and his two teenage sons, 15 and 16, filed to live with him rather than their "Wicked Witch of the North" mother who sued for custody.

That summer, my third friend Steve planned to ride his motorcycle to Alaska with several of us. But, of course, he found a new girlfriend in the spring named Paula.

He invited me over to meet her along with several other couples.

We spent several hours talking and socializing. I brought my girlfriend, too. During the afternoon, I finally got to talk with Paula and Steve. Great conversation and superb food! I spent a total of 20 minutes talking with Paula, of which, she commanded 19 minutes.

Losing Your Best Friend

A week before we prepared to shove off on our great Alaska bike adventure, Bob gave me a call.

"Hey dude," he said.

"Hey man," I said.

"This is probably no big deal," Steve said, "But during our conversation last week, Paula thinks that you think that she's dumb."

"What?" I gasped. "I didn't say anything; she did all the talking."

"It's no big deal," Steve said. "Oh, I can't go to Alaska. Paula and I are going backpacking in the Grand Canyon."

Steve never invited me over to his place again. He never called. He never answered my phone calls when I returned from the Alaska trip. I never saw him again. I wondered if I was the problem, but he did the same thing to two other buddies just like me.

It seems that his girl Paula didn't like us riding bikes or her man going on adventures with us. She shunned camping and the outdoors. She also turned out to be a couch potato, and consequently, she turned Steve into one, too.

In the dynamics of men and women, I discovered that if a friend's girlfriend or wife doesn't like you for whatever reason, even if you are a saint, no matter how many years of friendship—you're gone in a heartbeat. Your buddy will back up, back off and vanish from your life no matter how many great memories. If she does tolerate you, it will never be like it was. He'll come up with excuses, reasons or no word at all.

Some exceptions exist: a guy or gal might make a stand with a mate by introducing boundaries—to kindly avoid being henpecked or 'himpecked' to lessen one's individuality.

I've also discovered that the more dynamic you are or perhaps, the less dynamic, you better pray that your friend's wife enjoys her own personal security as a person. If not, she holds ultimate power over your friendship.

Chapter 7—
Losing friends with changing family situation

"A friend is a patient sounding board: listening, understanding, and then sharing genuine advice based on shared ideals. A friend is a courageous speaker of the truth at a time when it is most difficult to hear. A friend draws from the same well of life you do, and shines back on you a light to your own path."

Ken Hampshire

My friend Art, a man that I worked with at a company in Denver, shared a lot in common with me. We laughed through our tears at our situation within the company.

He responded to my stories about wives and girlfriends wrecking male friendships.

"More thoughts on friendship," Art said. "Your last line about girlfriends and wife's chasing away friends got me to ruminating about some of the "friends" that drifted away after my son Elliott was born.

"I had friends of over ten years running, who were childless by choice when Elliott was born.

"Jim, Roger and their wives were folks I knew back in Buffalo. They moved to Colorado after Pamela and I did. We all skied together, attended garden concerts and even tractor pulls together. Oh, they were thrilled when Elliott was born. They came to the christening, etc.

"As the years passed we saw less and less of them. We made it a point to see each other at Thanksgiving, but it just wasn't the same. Elliott was the only child in the room.

"I found that more and more of my friends were the fathers of Elliott's classmates, Boy Scouts or teammates.

"Whereas, with most true friends , we are willing to overlook some personality traits, I found myself holding back with the guys and listening to our conversation as if I were an outsider hiding in the room unseen.

"I became rather judgmental and started to see the guys as shallow and unfulfilled. They would talk about their new sports cars and I talked about teaching Elliott to ride the new bike. They talked about vacations in the south of France; I talked about Youth Baseball Camp in Phoenix.

"I suppose they found me boring, but I did spare them the excitement of potty training stories after all.

"The guys came to Elliott's graduation, gave him gifts. Elliott still calls them Uncle Jim and Uncle Roger.

"The guys made sure I had my season ski pass this year and want to see me on the slopes now that Elliott is away at college.

"To the guys, I'm back to being Art after an absence of 18 years. I don't know if I've changed, matured or am just plain old and tired, but I can't help but think that our friendship will never be what it once was."

Chapter 8—
Power of a friend for growth or change of life choices

"A best friend is a guy who is 'there' for you at your finest hour and your darkest moment."
Jonathan Jackson

You never know when an angel might sit on your shoulder or a friend may pop into your life. As Drew Chalker's poem states, some friends come into your life for a reason, season or a lifetime. I met my friend Doug at a youth hostel in Wellington, New Zealand on one of my bicycle journeys around the world. When you muscle up mountains and share hundreds of campfires, a tremendous bond establishes a rock solid friendship. We maintain our connection 25 years later.

But with my friend Ken, we met through a newspaper article written about my efforts to create a sustainable and stable population in America. He looked me up in the phone book after reading the article in the Denver Post. We had both attended MSU and enjoyed memories of our college years. In the last third of our lives, we became instant friends. He brought tremendous enthusiasm and wisdom to the table.

Ken related an amazing experience of the power of friendship, "College days really are like a kitchen blender—mix in hormones, fearlessness, ignorance, vitality, optimism, and all the other emotions that pulse through a 20-something's veins, and you will almost always get a memorable result! Mine came in my second semester of my freshman year in 1975 while studying for the ministry at a small Christian school in Indiana.

Ken related his story:

I came to college knowing what I wanted to do and be—a minister, a man who knew truth, who lived it, and would teach it. I knew about character and the importance of a man's word. My dad taught me that growing up on a dairy farm in mid-Michigan... like learning how to politely refuse money from a grateful traveler after knocking on our door late on a snowy night requesting help to get his car out of a ditch; or what not to say to a 15 year old son who, after nearly five years of responsible driving and handling of numerous trucks, tractors, and machines of all sorts, walked in the door of our small farm house and announced to everyone around the dinner table that he had just flipped the truck upside down in a small ditch while taking my grade school friend home after a long, hot day of baling hay; or, later, while away at college, being told by my older brother, how he and my dad had quietly unloaded loads of hay in our neighbor's yard at night so that our proud neighbor, who had just lost nearly everything in a barn fire, would not be able to pay for it, as he surely would have if he had known who left it.

These experiences, and countless others like it, all blended together in my young mind to form a strong sense of honesty and integrity, a gift from a dad to his son.

Surely, the ministry, more than any other occupation, was where honesty and integrity was found, and I immersed myself in its pursuit with all that I had.

Soon enough, word got out among some of the other students that I had some "promise." I was invited to leave the dorm at the end of my first semester to live with four other students, one sophomore, one junior, and two seniors in a five-man house respected campus-wide for intellectual and personal achievement. One of the students of "House 11" was to transfer out at the end of the semester, and they wanted me!

The next couple of years were to change my life. College often does that for young men and women, but this change was different.

I got to know Bruce, the unspoken leader of House 11, and we became good friends. He was brilliant, perhaps the most intelligent man I have met to this day. He possessed a rare gift of insight and wisdom that was many, many years past his, and my young age, that would take him into private discussions after hours with many of the college professors. It was easy to be taken in, at both his presence and his interest in me. He counseled me in what classes to take—history, philosophy, comparative religion, and we talked about the meaning of life late into many, many nights. I believed what he told me and trusted him with my life.

I was engaged to my high school sweetheart when I moved into House 11, but I was young and naïve. Unknowing to me, my life was being channeled into a narrow path with little room for change or awareness. In fact, ignoring life outside my particular belief structure was part of "living" the life I was being taught; you could observe life outside of the church, but you must always take care never to get caught up in it. I was like a train on its track, going wherever the track went with few questions or original thoughts. Little did I know how "unlike" House 11 philosophy my life was, but I was to soon find out!

One night after talking with Bruce, he looked straight at me and said, "Ken, your life is really messed up." He paused as he looked slightly away. He turned back. "With your permission, I'd like to take your life apart and put it back together again."

Just like that! Simple! Direct! I was clay in the sculptor's hands. I said, "Yes!"

It didn't take long for the fallout to start. One of the first things Bruce told me was that my engagement to my high school sweetheart was not right. He asked me, "If you don't even know who you are, how in the world can you expect to get married?"

In my mind I knew it was a real question and I was scared of the answer. We were playing for keeps here and I knew it.

I told my fiancée that I needed some time to learn about myself, my journey, my life. She was hurt badly but tried not to let it show. She said she understood, and while she knew my demands that this be permanent, so as to not sabotage the outcome, she would wait for me. My heart broke with humility at her acceptance of what I knew to be my own shortcomings. Yet she was willing to wait. What kind of love is that I wondered?

Life became a whirlwind of reading, study, discussion, and debate. Bruce taught me how to look beyond my own opinions, to see the motivations behind words and actions of those around me. I experienced a sensitivity I had never known as I learned about how alike we all are. I was becoming a realized person.

I absorbed knowledge by reading books, hundreds of them. I made an outline and kept a file of each one. My thinking grew larger as my world expanded through the writings of philosophers and theologians. Finally, as a sophomore in a senior level philosophy class, I received the highest grade for my semester final paper on the definition of ultimate knowledge. It was time for the student to break from the teacher.

It got more difficult for Bruce to answer my questions, or even to give counsel without becoming judgmental. While Bruce told me he was only "opening me to myself," and was usually careful to allow me to find my own way, some of his own personal beliefs were portrayed as being "truth." Some of these ran counter to my own, and I had reached a point where I no longer accepted everything Bruce said without question.

Our discussions grew more heated. Shorter, too! Feelings boiled to the surface. Finally, after an intense disagreement during a 10-day trip down the east coast, our friendship came to a close. The most intense friendship and learning experience of my life lasted a little over two years.

Long before my friendship with Bruce ended, I re-stated my love for my high school sweetheart and she was gracious enough to take me back. We were married April 2, 1977 and raised three wonderful children. We remained married until our divorce some 22 years later. She said she never forgave me for breaking our first engagement.

Friendships are intense and sometimes gut-wrenching experiences. I am now married to a beautiful and wonderful woman I love dearly.

Chapter 9— Best friend as a surrogate father

"A best friend can be separated for years but seems to be able to pick up the conversation from where he left off. You can listen to each other but can also hear what isn't being said."

Art Varga

When I grew up, I naturally leaned toward guys who showed me kindness or shared my sports interests.

Today, I present wild enthusiasm for life and in my relationships. I'm the first one to fire up on the dance floor with all the women and the last one to leave the floor. I'm excited to go skiing or climb that 14er. If it's a bicycle ride, I'm pedaling up that canyon road quicker than a hawk can snatch a prairie dog! Some can handle such energy while others recoil from it. You never quite know who finds your personality 'style' attractive or an annoyance.

However, I discovered that you cannot change yourself to fit somebody's need for you to be different or to fit his/her style. People need to find friends that fit their styles or energy levels.

I remember on my college floors when the wild guys raised all sorts of hell and quiet guys loved it. They witnessed exciting times. However, after college, those quiet guys returned to their sedate styles. Years later, they lamented as they recalled those days as the most exciting of their lives.

Whereas, the exciting guys stepped into life for even more exciting life paths!

When I reached Colorado, I walked into athletic heaven. I skied, biked, hiked, climbed, rafted, became a mountaineer, board sailed, ran triathlons, danced and much more.

Teaching math and science proved a great experience, but a beggar's salary kept me in the poor house. Therefore, each summer, I worked for United Van Lines as a long haul trucker.

My dispatcher, Tim, two years older than me, and an MSU graduate, offered me a 48 foot trailer, a big Ford truck and 18 wheels of money-making power each summer.

Tim, at 6'3" and 220, presented a humorous countenance. I liked him immediately. Plus, we enjoyed the connections we shared as Spartans. He organized my loads to all 48 states. He gave me my orders each day and I drove over to the residences and loaded them. Once I loaded 20,000 pounds of household goods, I drove that rig to Dallas, Los Angeles, Chicago, Miami, Seattle and New York.

The job proved sweaty, brutal, 100 hour weeks and thousands of miles of endless boredom—driving the rig. But I found myself working for big money and to please him.

Losing Your Best Friend

I called him daily to keep him up to date with my progress of unloading or loading a shipment. Each call, we shared a joke or story or something about past girlfriends. Every Monday, I popped into the dispatch office ready for another load assignment.

After the summer, I invited him to ski, to backpack on weekends or attend football games. To my chagrin, he never responded in the affirmative. I called him often during the nine months I taught school. I sent him my annual Christmas letter.

Each summer, I found myself trying to please him. He always told me that I had completed a good move with Mr. Jones or Mrs. Smith. I lapped up that praise even though he was my equal.

As you may remember, I lost my father at 17. It left a gargantuan hole in my emotional makeup. Where my father used to tell me how proud he was of me, I no longer enjoyed a father to be proud of me.

Unknown known to me, I slowly regarded Tim as my surrogate father. At summer's end, I bought him substantial gifts. I once bought him a Buck knife with a personal engraving on it attesting our friendship. He never mentioned it.

On my world travels, I sent him gifts from China, Japan, South America and Australia. I wrote funny stories from all four corners of the planet. I sent him cards and called him on his birthday every year. I wished him Merry Christmas every year for 20 years.

Finally, my first book published. I sent him a copy.

No response! No congratulations! No nothing!

I remained dumbfounded after a few weeks. Surely he honored that having my first book published constituted my highest life goal! Without a doubt, he must be proud of me!

Nope! Didn't faze him enough to call or write a congratulations card!

While he always responded to my calls, he never participated in my life whatsoever.

Then it hit me right between the eyes! He only enjoyed my attention toward him as long as I made all the effort. He was never my best friend nor even a friend. He considered me one of his drivers; his employee. He didn't care one iota about my life other than when I talked to him. And, he never shared anything about his life. I used to ask him. His reply, "Same ole same ole." In fact, he had gotten a divorce without me knowing it.

After 20 years, I changed agencies for my summer job with United. I wrote Tim asking why he hadn't acknowledged my gift of my first and second books to him.

No response! Nothing!

He didn't care, couldn't care or didn't have the emotional equipment to carry on a friendship, or at least a friendship with me. My mind or emotions created our 'best friendship'. My emotional needs 'made' him my friend because I needed him to be proud of me, i.e., like a father. Thus, I created a surrogate dad.

Tim couldn't be faulted! He didn't have a clue that I had made him my best friend. Tim enjoyed me when I stood near him, but once out of sight, to him, out of mind. Looking back, I bet he enjoyed his friends in his own realm. I'll bet his best friend remains as dear to him as mine.

But I wasn't his friend.

After I didn't receive a word from him, I decided to give him as much as he gave me: nothing!

I never heard from again.

But I did learn from the experience. We all want our fathers and mothers to be proud of us. If we don't have a father or mother, many of us create a 'surrogate' parent to fulfill that need.

After I realized what I had done with Tim, I decided to be proud of myself. At the same time, I am thankful that Tim provided me that 'surrogate' father image while he didn't even realize it.

Life and friendships, indeed, move forward in mysterious ways.

Chapter 10—
Spirit friends versus casual friends

"True friendship is like sound health; the value of it is seldom known until it is lost."
Charles Caleb Colton

That brings me to this concept of 'spirit friendship'.
I've played racquetball all my life since college. I love the speed, sweat and passion of the game. I love the sheer exhilaration of winning and losing the contest. I love the total 'satori' of it or 'perfect moment'. When I'm on the court, I am fully present in the here and now. There's no yesterday and no tomorrow. There's only that little blue ball whizzing around the court at 100 miles per hour—and you've got to hit it before it bounces twice.

I've played hundreds of guys in tournaments and challenge courts in my life. I've played on teams. Nothing bonds two men more than the struggle in that sports arena.

However, I've played many of them a hundred times or more, but no connection or friendship resulted.

Yet, at certain points in my life, I met guys one time and we became friends for life. Why? That's an intriguing question.

Have you ever met some guy at church, school, sports contest or a business meeting—and instantly liked him? You felt his good vibrations.

But more than the compatibilities, something about his spirit moved you. At least, for me, some of my life-long friends possessed a spiritual aspect that infused me with attraction for them.

A spirit friend remains, oh so rare! Oh so indefinable! Oh so mysterious as to how the connection happens!

I've enjoyed several in my lifetime:

On a bicycle trip from Sydney, Australia on my way to Melbourne, a guy drove by in a red car with a sports rack on top. He pulled over, jumped out and walked back to me.

"How ya'goin' mate?" he said, extending his hand. "I'm John Brown from Kiama."

"Frosty Wooldridge, Denver, Colorado," I said, shaking his hand.

"Where you headed on your push-bike?" he asked.

"Down the Princess Highway to Melbourne and on to Ceduna up the Great Ocean Road," I said.

"You got time to stop at my place about 20 kilometers from here?" he said. "I'll offer you shower, dinner and a beer with me mates."

"Sure," I said.

"Oh, and here are the keys to my place," he said. "I've got to coach a swim class and won't be home till later. And, stop at the "Fantastic Fruit and Veggie Stand" to pick up directions and food from the owner."

With that one single happenstance meeting, John Brown and I have remained best friends on two different continents for over 25 years. And, we bicycled coast to coast across America and border to border.

These many years later, I watched him suffer divorce, loss of parents, nearly lose his own life to cancer and other challenges. John chose some different turns in his spiritual life, but through it all, we've enjoyed a spiritual connection that continues to the present moment.

Another fellow sat at a table in Wellington, New Zealand with his bicycle gear spread out as he organized it.

"How goes it mate?" I asked.

"Good," he said. "You traveling south?"

"Sure am," I said. "All the way to Invercargill."

"Need a partner?" he said.

"Sure," I said. "Let's ride."

Since that meeting, he's traveled across seven continents. I bicycled across the USA once with him, the length of South America and down the Continental Divide. The most amazing world traveler I've ever met, Doug Armstrong and I have been lifelong friends for 25 years. At the same time, others that rode with me on those epic rides never remained connected after the tour. They didn't take time to respond to my Christmas cards. They ignored the friendship. It died!

Losing Your Best Friend

At my orientation for Antarctica, I snapped a few pictures and scribbled notes for what I knew would be a fantastic book from my living and working 'on the ice' at the South Pole.

A red-haired, tall, lean smiling dude approached me, "You must be Frosty!"

From that moment on, of all the people in Antarctica who proved some of the most amazing adventure seekers on the planet, and whom I befriended—only one of them, Sandy Colhoun, became one of my best friends for life.

In Antarctica, he worked as editor of the Antarctic Sun while I wrote weekly columns. As photographers and writers, we hit it off in an amazingly spiritual way at the bottom of the planet!

I worked in his office each day pounding the keyboard while he shot pictures and wrote feature stories. As an athlete, he ran road races, sailed and bicycled. We related on every level.

Many years after stepping off the ice, we keep in touch. We call; we write; and we email. Whereas, all the rest of those amazing people slipped into memories! Why?

Spirit friends share something not defined by the books, DVDs, lectures or even human understanding. Call it a 'soul' connection or a shared spiritual union of mind and body—something intangible but lasting!

Another man wrote about living in Colorado where he met another man on the tennis court in Golden, "Gateway to the Rockies." Ron described Al as very tall, lean, fast, quick and could kick butt! Easy smile! Firm handshake! Hell of a backhand!

Al taught English at a local high school.

He liked to climb, bicycle and camp. His wife, however, remained a couch potato, terribly overweight, insecure and bossy. Which, unfortunately, created an interesting conundrum for him and his friendships.

Yet, he also proved very affectionate.

It's odd that some of his friends gave him a big hug when they saw him while others extended their hands for the usual handshake. Ron never quite figured out the reasons, but each man expresses emotions in his own way.

Do you know the original reason for the handshake? It's quite interesting. In order to prove you didn't carry a weapon such as a knife and later, a gun, western societies evolved with the man extending his hand. That gesture proved the man didn't carry a weapon. Thus, the 'handshake'!

Al gave Ron a hug every time he saw him. Just his style! Ron enjoyed other friendships with never a hug, ever.

As spirit friends, Ron hung out with Al for 22 years with one of the best friendships he had ever encountered. They climbed Colorado's 14,000 peaks, trained and raced in triathlons and spent a lot of time in the weight room. Ron adored Al's three kids. But in a blink, his wife destroyed it because he and Al expressed more affections and enjoyed more fun than the two of them together. More on that in a later chapter! (Broken friendships by outside factors)

Losing Your Best Friend

On a bicycle tour in Colorado 20 years ago, I bonded with a man named Jack. While eating breakfast in Golden, about 10 miles from Denver on I-70, a man walked into the restaurant wearing bicycle garb.

"Where you headed?" he asked.

"Over to Aspen, on tour!" I said.

"Mind if I ride along?" he said.

As you can imagine, when someone rides a bicycle up 12,000 foot passes in Colorado, that's my kind of guy. Gutsy! Physical! Outdoor-type that doesn't complain when it's hot or cold! No matter how rough the adventure, he gets down the road.

Jack and I shared a lot of ourselves and our life philosophies on our way over 11,000 foot Loveland Pass.

After he departed for a meeting in Vail, I continued on my way over 11,318 Freemont Pass to Aspen. Later, we met for skiing that winter.

Soon, motorcycle trips to Glacier, raft trips down the Grand Canyon and, of course, I invited him into the dance world. He became a championship dancer. Women flocked to him. He thanked me for adding dancing to his world experiences.

As usual, we shared several bicycle touring adventures. We motorcycled 10,000 miles to Alaska. We bicycled from the Arctic Circle, Norway to Athens, Greece over 3,500 miles. Those grand adventures created an incredible friendship, or so I thought.

We always shook hands because he wasn't the 'show affection' type. No problem! Everybody expresses a different style.

Then, one day, he ended our friendship without so much as a word of explanation. More on that later!

While taking language classes in French in St. Foy, Quebec, I met Denis on the racquetball court. Oh man, we shared heated battles on the court, but once off the court, we hit the ski slopes, danced with the ladies and shared bicycle adventures.

Over the years, we shared trucking, XC skiing, backpacking, bicycle touring down the Continental Divide (Book: Bicycling the Continental Divide: Slice of Heaven, Taste of Hell), and across Europe.

Over those years, I've enjoyed his wife, family, friends and personal successes. He and I have continued our friendship nearly 30 years. Denis and I enjoy 'spirit friendship'. For the past 30 years, we have called each other on our birthdays.

If you're lucky enough to enjoy a 'spirit friendship', few greater miracles enter a man's or a woman's life. When you 'happen' into one of them, take care to enjoy it for every second, every adventure moment and every precious life-fulfilling, memory- making aspect of it.

That 'spirit' part of such a friendship revolves around chemistry, shared adventures, day to day contact and integrity. If you lose one of them, either by another person's actions or your own mistakes—you'll lament the day depending on your own emotional makeup.

Chapter 11—
Losing a best friend to his best friend: booze

"He's there for you, thick and thin, he's there for you. You know you can count on him; that's my best friend."
                                                        Bob Johannes

Because my father and mother didn't drink, I grew up clueless as to the effects of alcohol. I didn't know what it did. I didn't know about its effects and I never saw my dad angry, crazy or drunk.

About the time I hit 14, my military father spent 18 months overseas in Japan. My mom and we four kids stayed at our farm in central Michigan. Across the road, my grandfather milked 50 head of cows, planted corn, wheat and alfalfa. I discovered the gift of common sense and hard work for the next two summers and winters.

I also found out about booze and drunks. My Uncle Scott drank like a fish. He beat his dog, his wife and the cows. He took a board to the cows if they didn't move into the right spot for him—to be milked. He whipped his dog "Pouchie" at his slightest drunken whim.

I couldn't quite get a handle on it because he seemed to be the same man before he became drunk, but then, he slurred his words and didn't make any sense. His nose suffered a bunch of blood vessels running like spider webs. Alcohol causes bleeding ulcers, puffy skin, expanded pores, spider veins in a man's nose and bloodshot eyes.

Uncle Scott finally received a gut shot with a 12 gauge shotgun from his other drunken friend as they argued over the size of a window during a Saturday afternoon drinking binge. That's about all they discovered as to the meaning of life—at the bottom of a bottle.

Not only Scott, but his brother Jake! Talk about a happy drunk! Jake drank before driving, while driving and after driving a pickup truck down the road. Luckily, he drove 30 miles an hour on country roads. However, he raged, yelled and made a complete ass of himself that embarrassed his wife if they ever spent time with friends.

Once, he chased me around our farmhouse to teach me a lesson. I ran away from him not knowing what he might do. Finally, he ran out of breath and his wife drove him home. He couldn't remember the incident the next week when I saw him. His brain, by age 50, suffered extreme deterioration.

At 52, he came over for something that I couldn't remember.

"How you doin' Uncle Jake?" I asked.

"Well, Frosty, I've smoked a pack of cigarettes and drank a six pack of beer and it ain't even noon yet," he said, coughing. "Other than a touch of cancer, I'm feelin' great!"

He roared with laughter, but several months later, the doctors diagnosed lung cancer. He died shortly thereafter leaving three kids and a widow.

I felt sorry for Uncle Jake, but I felt worse for my cousins. Alcoholics don't have a clue as to the misery they bring their loved ones.

Remembering Uncle Scott, I loathed the man. His meanness repelled and sickened me. I learned to stay away from him.

One day, my mother became angry at me. I hadn't done my chores or something.

"You're going to be just like your Uncle Scott," she yelled at me.

I turned to her, "I will never be like my Uncle Scott!" I said. "I will never drink like that low-life creep."

To this day, other than a glass of wine at special parties, I can't stand alcohol. When I think of all the misery it has caused men and their families, along with death and mayhem on our highways, I am sickened at the effects of alcohol on our society.

But as you can tell from this story from my long time friend Bob, alcohol can become a greater friend than your best friend.

Bob wrote: Out of the blue came the question, "Bob, why don't you become the social chairman of the house?"

The 'house' was the Sigma Chi fraternity at Michigan State University. The 'questioner' was Jerry.

My first reaction was this guy Jerry has thought about my talents and placed faith in me. My second thought was to give this guy Jerry another look. In that flash of time grew a friendship which continues to this day even though Jerry is gone from this life, a victim of alcoholism.

My wife Marie and I maintained contact with Jerry's wife Gwen and her husband George after Jerry's passing. Recently Gwen and George came to visit us in Colorado. As Marie, Gwen and George stood in the kitchen, I came down the stairs from the second floor wanting to ask a question of George. But, "Jerry" came out of my mouth and in unison all three replied, "It's George not Jerry!" They all know that Jerry still lives in my life.

In college Jerry saw a summer job ad and suggested we apply. We did but unfortunately Jerry didn't get selected due to problems with his hips. He went home for the summer to work in the parks of Chicago while I went to Midland, Michigan and found another friend.

Jerry was there at the Coral Gables when I met my wife of 40 years on her 21st birthday. Jerry and I lived together in an apartment in downtown Lansing our senior year. As Marie and I got serious, she spent many weekends at the apartment with Jerry and me.

Shortly after we married, Marie realized it was Jerry that was the real jokester in our little threesome.

After college Jerry met Gwen and marriage followed soon thereafter. With his law degree, Jerry was off to a solid future in the northern suburbs of Chicago. Our two families spent at least one holiday together every year. We gathered back at the fraternity house for fall football every year. And there was always a chess match between Jerry and me.

But as time went on, Jerry's best friend became alcoholic. It cost him his job, his family and finally his life. He was never able to stop drinking for long. There aren't many days that go by without my wondering why? "Why did my best friend get this burden to carry? Why was there nothing that I or anyone could say or do to change that destructive force in his life? How did I not come to that same end?

Last year, Marie and I went to Jerry and Gwen's son Tommy's wedding. Tom only knew Jerry at his worst as alcoholism took a hold of his life. Tommy wanted to know about his father before the downward spiral began. So he and his new wife Lindsay came to visit us.

Strange that his first question was, "What was my father's favorite color?"

I replied, "That I might not know his favorite colors but I do know his favorite food was a boiled hot dog on a lightly buttered toasted slice of bread for a bun. That was the only food we kept around the apartment. His favorite beverage was three beers between 5 and 6 p.m. chilled to the point of freezing on ice covered with rock salt in Jim Fickey's room on the third floor of the Sigma Chi house.

The open ended questions continued throughout the day. And my answers covering the smallest details of a friend's life, to help fill in a hazy picture in a son's mind about his father, continued.

I miss laughing with Jerry. I miss his sharp wit. I miss playing chess with Jerry. I miss talking sports with Jerry. I'm sad he is gone from this life. I'm sad he died alone after trying once again to kick the alcohol habit. I'm sorry someone with so much promise of a successful life didn't get to see the fine man his son became.

But I'm glad he is part of my life and I knew his promising future in his prime.

After hearing Bob's story about his friend, I asked Bob why didn't he try to 'talk' with Jerry to help him out of drinking.

"Everybody tried to stop Jerry from drinking," Bob said. "Once I drove to Chicago after his wife divorced him. He rented an apartment that was trashed. He had me sleep on the front room sofa. That night, I was awakened at midnight from him picking at the ice block in the freezer to fill a mug with ice. It happened again at 2 a.m. and again at 4 a.m. The next morning, I opened the fridge to see rows of bottles of Scotch. He couldn't help himself. He died at 55."

Chapter 12—
Losing a best friend by outside factors

"Losing your best friend rips at your guts like a dagger cutting you deeper than you ever thought possible, leaving you with an ache that lingers for many years."
A friend who lost a friend

A friend at church asked if he could write his special story in order to share his grief about losing his best friend.

Ron said, "How do you speed through 22 years of friendship faster than an alarm clock can ring in the morning? It's like you hit the sack at 9:00 p.m., and you're already out of bed to hit the shower a moment later. Where did nine hours of sleep go so fast?

As discussed in Chapter 6, a wife or girlfriend can break up your friendship, but you cannot imagine it happening in your 40s or 50s when most folks mellow out.

Ron described such a story: My friend Al and I formed our friendship after 35. Those mornings on the tennis court, with the sun rising and a cool breeze, etched into our minds with vivid memories of laughter, great plays, defeat and victory.

After tennis, we enjoyed breakfast at the Golden Breakfast Nook. He talked about his students and fellow teachers. I talked about my teaching stories.

He talked a lot about his frustrations with his wife. When he married her, she enjoyed a reasonable weight. While he enjoyed athletics and great physical prowess, she quickly became a couch potato who loved to bake cookies—then, proceed to eat all of them. Her body responded by looking like one of those 'starting' contestants on the TV show, "Biggest Losers."

With three daughters and five years into the marriage, he felt lost.

"Why don't you two go see a counselor?" I said.

"We have, but our relationship is like a ball of yarn that's so knotted up that you can't find where to start, and if you do, you find more knots than you can untie to get to the problem," Al said.

Al talked of her tremendous frustration at being very intelligent and highly educated, but she couldn't control her eating problems. She desperately wanted to be attractive, but couldn't stop eating. Not only that, he said her interest in sex rivaled that of a 90 year old woman. He took cold showers and read a lot of Playboy.

When I first met Marge, she struck me as being defensive and insecure. Al called her the "Ayatollah" after the Ayatollah Komanei of Iran who took over as an absolute dictator.

When I visited after tennis or a mountain climbing weekend, she nit-picked him to death. He defended as best he could. She didn't seem to mind embarrassing him in front of me and other guests. His other friends who watched the behavior felt sorry for Al.

At one point during an argument, in front of their three girls, she attacked and punched Al nearly knocking him to the floor. By 10 years into the marriage, she outweighed him."

Later, he told me, "Marge told me to find Christian friends."

"What did I do to deserve that comment?" I asked.

"Nothing," Al responded. "Don't worry about it. She's just angry about everything."

Accordingly, I kept out of Marge's way. However, Al's three girls loved Uncle Ron and wanted to go camping with us. Marge's idea of camping remained the honeymoon suite at the Marriot as long as sex wasn't expected.

As I heard more and more of Al's complaints, I found out that Marge possessed more hang-ups than a Burlington coat factory. I ached for him, but as long as we spent time climbing, skiing and playing golf along with our love of bicycling—our friendship blossomed.

Luckily, he could express his frustrations to me, which kept him balanced and sane. Lonely self-love in the shower became his main sex life.

As the years passed, Al and I enjoyed two mountain climbing weekends every summer. We finished 40—14ers or 14,000 foot peaks. He always invited her, but no go. She wouldn't even watch him come into the finish of a triathlon. Marge never participated, but did shop, eat and shop. I think she hated him because he was so physically fit and her size embarrassed herself as well as him in public.

The more fun Al and I enjoyed together, the madder and madder she became.

She validated the adage by Anne Lindbergh, "If one is estranged from oneself, then one is estranged from others, too. If one is out of touch with oneself, then one cannot touch others."

Over the years, she demanded to know where he was at all times. He started asking for permission to play tennis with me or go on a bike ride.

"Al, for heaven sakes," I said. "You shouldn't have to beg your wife to go play tennis at 5:30 a.m. on a Saturday morning. Hell, it's not like you're getting two hours of sex on Saturdays. At least you're getting two hours of tennis!"

While he still called her "the Ayatollah", I didn't hear any affectionate ring to it any more.

After 20 years, I watched Al transform from a man who enjoyed life, to a man beaten by life. Marge controlled him. She spent all his money on everything that would pile up in the house and then, give it to the Salvation Army. She couldn't stop buying 'things'. She scowled a lot. She ate often.

Two of his girls became sullen as if taking after their mother. The other started gaining weight by age 11, lots of weight.

One day Al said, "If I divorce her, she'll hurt me by taking the girls and I'll lose my family."

"Got no answers," I said. "Your girls are acting out the drama they see between you two. Maybe family counseling would help."

In the spring of our 20th year of friendship, we finished playing a spirited tennis match. He won!

As we walked back to the cars, Al said, "You know that Marge thinks you disrespect her for being overweight."

"Good grief man," I said. "I haven't seen her for eight weeks. How could she come up with a charge like that?"

"She also thinks you are a know-it-all," Al said.

"Good heavens man," I said. "I'm a teacher, so I teach about everything happening in the US and around the world. Am I supposed to be a deaf-mute to make her happy? I haven't had a conversation with her for heaven sakes!"

"Ah, don't worry about it," Al said.

Another aspect of our friendship stemmed from the fact that Al liked to hug people. He and I always hugged when we met each other. Just a big old bear hug! But Marge didn't like that either! Ironically, Al and Marge enjoyed a king-sized bed, but Al said that they slept as far apart as possible. She wasn't into cuddling or touching.

Into that spring, Al started acting funny-weird. He brought up that his wife felt that I condemned her for being overweight, again. He told her that my idea of them going to family counseling pissed her off.

"Al," I said. "For heaven sakes, I don't condemn anyone for being overweight. I haven't seen her in three months and I've never mentioned an inkling of that subject to her in the past 22 years. What the hell is going on?"

"Just problems, well, you know, the Ayatollah on the war path," Al said.

"Let me go talk with her with you present to assure her that I am not a shallow bastard that condemns anyone for being overweight," I said.

"No, she doesn't want to be confronted by you," Al said.

"Hey man, you've never heard me ever say anything about her weight," I said.

"I know," Al said.

"I feel like I'm being tried and convicted of something that I haven't said or done," I said. "How about if I never come over to your house again so she can't dream this shit up?"

"Ah, don't worry about it," Al said.

At the time, I enjoyed a girlfriend and, as bad luck would have it, we attended a party at the Rose Cowboy Bar in Golden where Marge and Al also attended by bad luck of fate.

Being accomplished dancers, my gal Paula and I put on a dance show at the party. At 5'10" and possessing a dancer's body, any of the party-goers could see we enjoyed dancing with West Coast Swing, Cha Cha and Salsa. Anyone at the party could see the sparks flying!

That became the worst night of my life. That's when I lost my best friend Al.

Two days later, I received a letter in the mail from Al. It explained how we had different values and we were headed in different directions. I could 'see' the

Losing Your Best Friend

Ayatollah literally holding the tip of a dagger on the back of his hand while he wrote the letter.

It showed me the ultimate power of a wife in terms of controlling her husband's friendships—and life for that matter. She changed him from a man into a mouse. And, while she took total control over him, it angered her further that he wasn't a man any longer.

I think she liked her dominance, but she hated him for letting her become the 'man' in the family. Heck of a love/hate relationship!

Enjoying an affectionate friend like me angered her more than she could stand.

In the end, I forgave her because her pain ran deep and his pain ran deeper. Whatever her mental torture, I wouldn't trade for her personal anguish in a lifetime of Sundays. And for my best friend Al, may his journey climb from the depths to the light as he moves through his life.

Ron's story repeats itself all over America in every realm of male and female interactions. Unfortunately, millions of relationships stagger through the years like Al's, but mostly, you see smiles masking their anguished lives. While 50 percent of marriages end in divorces, another 25 percent do not divorce—but live with the anger, pain and agony.

What happened to Ron? He's a pretty cool guy and still paints the dance floor with Paula and a whole lot of passion!

Chapter 13—
Losing a friend via unwanted advice

"No love, no friendship, can cross the path of our destiny without leaving some mark on it forever."
                                   Francois Mocuriac

Jack! What can you say about a man who has it all: James Bond tall, brilliant smile, rich, smart, athletic, creative, musical and enjoys an infectiously engaging personality?! Not only that, Jack "The Patrick Swayze of Dirty Dancing" fame lifts every woman to cloud nine on the dance floor.

First time I met the man, I liked him. The fact that he pedaled his bike to a conference in Vail over 100 miles showed me a man of true grit.

He dressed first class in the boardroom and wore hiking boots and camped with the aplomb of Daniel Boone.

He enjoyed more talents in his mind and body than a room filled with 1000 men.

I'll never forget that day I met him. I rode my touring bicycle 'Condor' up Clear Creek Canyon along raging white water. High vertical cliffs rose toward a cobalt sky. The water energized and the altitude invigorated. I headed my touring bike from Denver to Aspen, Colorado through the fall foliage. Gold! I struck visual gold. Changing aspen trees exploded around every curve! With such a brilliant ride, only good things could happen to me.

In Golden, I ate breakfast at a local diner. Later, before saddling up, I squatted to read the latest news in the paper box outside the restaurant.

"Need any help?" a voiced behind me called.

"Just catching the latest news," I said, looking around at a rugged dude on a road bike.

"Where you headed?" Jack asked.

"Over to Aspen on tour!" I said.

"Mind if I ride along?" Jack said.

"Sure," I said. "Frosty's my name."

"Jack," he said, extending his hand.

Thus began one of the most amazing friendships in my life. If not for meeting Jack, I would never have rafted the Grand Canyon on the Colorado River. If not for Jack, I would never have navigated a sailboat. If not for Jack, I wouldn't have met Pasquale Scaturro who climbed Everest three times, and guided the first blind man to summit the world's tallest mountain. If not for Jack, I would never have become involved with becoming an 18 year volunteer ski instructor for the handicapped at the National Sports Center for the Disabled in Winter Park, Colorado.

From one chance meeting, my whole life changed in amazing ways. It goes to show you that everything you do, counts! Every thought you bring into the universe stands in the "Law of Attraction" and your actions and energy create in that quantum field an amazing emotional energy field for others to enter. And, for you to enter into their energy fields!

We happily cranked the pedals five hours that day as we rode along the river. At the tunnel on I-70 they didn't allow cyclists so we turned left onto Route 6 over 11,300 foot Loveland Pass.

Jack joined the military and saw the world. He played a banjo and wrote incredible poetry. He competed in duathlons and talked about his 20,000 foot climbs in Mexico. He skied the Swiss Alps and motorcycled to Alaska. He rafted wild rivers like the Beo-Beo in Chile and the Selway, Green, Yampa and the Colorado through the Grand Canyon.

I liked being with him so much that I gave him my business card and eagerly grabbed his when we parted in Frisco. He continued on to Vail while I turned south toward Leadville.

A week later, we hooked up for a canyon ride. After that, we climbed a 14er. He invited me to a party where his friend invited me to become a volunteer ski instructor for the handicapped in Winter Park.

Every time I got together with Jack, something amazing happened.

In 17 years, we made extraordinary adventures on motorcycles and bicycles around the world. We danced more women around the floor than Patrick Swazye, Fred Astaire and Gene Kelly combined!

During all that time, not a sour word between us. Not an argument! Not even a trifling of a disagreement.

Losing Your Best Friend

Two peas in a pod would define how well we got along. He always spoke on the bright side of life.

About five years into our friendship, he hooked up with a fabulous lady named Melodie. She sported a body to die for, brains and beauty to match. Plus, funny! Great combination for him!

I have never seen a man full of more passion that Jack enjoyed with his fantasy woman. For one year, he met her in Vegas, Miami and Dallas. He made love, wrote poems and burst with excitement and sheer infatuation. Few men live a lifetime like that one year of fervor that Jack lived.

But, she broke his heart and left him for another man with more money, or more of something. I couldn't quite figure out how or why she left him because I knew him as a most incredible man. He suffered a bucket full of pain, but still carried the torch for her.

He kept in touch with her mother.

But nothing happened.

Then, he met a dancer, Nancy, and asked her to marry him. I stood as his best man at the wedding. The one thing that bothered me about the wedding stemmed from his being 13 years older than the bride. I told him my concern early on in his relationship.

"From now on," he said, "just give me your positive energy for this relationship."

I complied and never said another concerned word. I cried with joy at the wedding as he said, "I do!"

Couldn't have been nicer for Nancy and Jack to dance their lives away on the dance floor of life!

Another season of winter arrived. Every two weeks that ski season, we taught handicapped students together. Additionally, I saw Nancy and him at our dance club most Sunday nights. Jack and I called on the phone several times a week.

But things didn't seem right with him as he stopped talking. He entered a quiet period. No phone calls!

"You don't talk much anymore," I said one day at his condo after a day of teaching handicapped skiers.

"Things on my mind," he said.

"I'm here to listen any time you need to talk."

"Thanks," he said.

About three years later, his wife walked out of their home never to return.

Then, he called up his old flame, but she was with another man.

So, he began dating a gal named Janet. Nice gal! Athletic, built and down to earth.

He spent three years with her.

But on the side, he carried on with Melodie. Finally, Janet became very angry when she found out.

Jack left town to hook up with Melodie in another state. Janet suffered horrible loss of love. She cried her eyes out and suffered emotional trauma.

In the meantime, he didn't call me anymore. I figured he was up to his ears in passion.

But he did keep contacting Janet with emails and phone calls. Then, she called me up telling me how much pain she was having from his calls and emails.

Losing Your Best Friend

Like a damned emotional fool, I emailed Jack asking him to stop calling and emailing Janet to allow her to heal from losing him.

As soon as I emailed that note, that ended our friendship. He never talked to me again. He never wrote again. He never attempted to talk it out. I tried calling, writing emails and snail mail letters. I apologized all over myself.

For months, I fretted, cried and suffered depression.

Finally, I wrote him a closure letter to end the friendship officially.

Never heard a word!

After all those incredible years of shared adventures on the dance floor of life, he shut down like a guillotine.

Ironically, his 'fantasy woman' shut him down, too, and she went back to her old boy friend. Jack came back with hat in hand to Janet. She took him back.

In the end, I lost my best friend because I defended Janet, whom, in the end, he took back into his life.

My, how strange life becomes! Had I kept my mouth shut, I might still be best friends with Jack. I really didn't condemn him for two-timing Janet, because I know sex and passion trump common sense and ethics in the heat of ardor, but, as an emotional person, I tried to do the right thing.

It cost me, but, in the end, it cost Jack too, because he lost his best and most loyal friend in me.

Is there a moral to this story? Can we help ourselves during times of emotional turmoil? Perhaps if you talked to Jack, you would get a whole different story. Every saga finds two sides.

Whatever or whomever's story, two men lost the best friends of their lives. It proved tragic when you realize how much and how long it takes to build a close friendship. It takes time, shared experiences and that magic of chemistry that bonds two men who enjoy sharing each other's company.

I guess the only thing you can do is be true to your own morals and ethics. If you make mistakes, and we all do, we hope that our friends understand.

For certain, each human being on this planet enjoys a capricious ride through his or her life. We can do all the right things and still get our emotional, physical and spiritual butts kicked. If we could reach out with our tongue to lasso a few words or change directions with our actions—our lives might not suffer so much.

Yet for Jack, I wish him greater joy on his life path. I am thankful for the time we shared. I celebrate his life as he intertwined with mine. I raise a glass filled with life and photo albums always showing smiles from our triumphs on mountain tops, at the end of bike rides or the applause from attention on the dance floor of life. It doesn't get any better than sharing it with your best friend!

Chapter 14—
Possible reasons for friendship and compatibilities

"A friend is a person with whom I may be sincere. Before him I may think aloud. I am arrived at last in the presence of a man so real and equal, that I may drop even those undermost garments of dissimulation, courtesy, and second thought, which men never put off, and may deal with him with the simplicity and wholeness with which one chemical atom meets another."
                    Ralph Waldo Emerson

You may be interested in a behavior concept initiated via "Enneagram", the understanding that human beings fit into nine different and distinct personality categories as far as life motivations. Once born into one through nine on the Enneagram scale, your life moves along those lines as defined by that group.

For instance, highly energetic, expressive people cannot turn themselves into quiet, introverts. Their 'essence' demands expression. Whereas, introverted types cannot become effervescent. They usually won't stand up and give grand speeches. It's not in their nature. However, depending on environment and personal dynamics, anyone can alter their life paths by personal choices.

Helen Palmer stands out as a pre-imminent teacher. Visit her website, www.enneagram.com , for more information:

"The Enneagram is a highly sophisticated system of nine personality profiles set in a non-denominational framework compatible with contemporary psychological categories and spiritual traditions. It is meant to help us know ourselves, understand the people in our lives, and develop our relationships to the greater realities of spiritual experience. 'Ennea' simply means nine in Greek, and 'grammos' is something written or drawn. Arranged on a nine point diagram, the Enneagram personality types are identical to those used in psychological counseling and spiritual direction."

When you look back on Greek literature, you cannot help find the greats like Aristotle and Socrates.

"The Enneagram is far more than a hot new pop psych system that shows us how to get along with people who are motivated very differently from ourselves. In the pages that follow, you will see how the Enneagram functions as a road map to higher personal and spiritual integration for different types of people."

When you peruse the website, it will make sense to you as you apply it to yourself and watch others operate within their own lives.

"With a history of centuries, the Enneagram is arguably the oldest human development system on the

Losing Your Best Friend

planet. During the past decade, the system has undergone a renewal of scholarly attention within the context of current personality typologies. The result is a reliable integration of psychological insight about human differences, set alongside a non-sectarian body of spiritual practice that relaxes inner resistance while encouraging inner receptivity."

Finally, you can answer questions from the website to find out your own category!

"Each of the nine Enneagram personality profiles has a distinct, well-developed coping strategy for relating to self, others and the environment. Each of the nine types also has its own precise path to psychological and spiritual freedom."

Those nine groups include:

> The Perfectionist
> The Giver
> The Performer
> The Tragic Romantic
> The Observer
> The Loyal Skeptic
> The Epicure
> The Protector
> The Mediator

Each category enjoys strengths and weaknesses. This writer sports a solid '7' named "The Epicure"; always moving toward adventure, positive experiences and zest for life. Also, impulsive, does not want limits and possesses an inordinate amount of energy. Objective to a few!

As per the Enneagram system, certain persons easily enjoy compatibility while others avoid such persons at all costs.

Another study titled "Meyers-Briggs" offers why some people get along while others can't stand each other. The study shows four compatibility categories for men and women to consider if they plan for marriage. Those points revolve around: introverts, extroverts, feelers, non-feelers, intuitive sensors, perceptive and judgers, etc.

From my viewpoint, if a man and woman match in all four, they easily get along, don't fight, and fit together like two peas in a pod. If they enjoy three out of four compatible categories, they're still in good shape for long term compatibility.

However, when they share only two compatibilities or one—their relationship follows a rocky road of arguments or disinterest in the other person. If married, most end up in divorce or long, tenuous and benignly tolerant relationships. The majority slog onward for 'the kids' without understanding the 'why' of their unhappy or indolent lives.

However, these four compatibility markers don't necessarily hold true in all cases. Some folks with no matches enjoy lifelong positive relationships. For some, they might have to 'work' at a relationship whereas, those well matched, may enjoy 'playing' at their relationship.

One other point! You might think your best friend or friends would love your other best friends. But again, they may not match the criteria so one of your best friends could care less about your other friend.

It's just not in the cards. That's why 'married couple' friendships prove the hardest in the world. All it takes is one incompatible person in a couple 'situation' and it won't work.

Barbara DeAngelis wrote a brilliant book along those lines: **Are You the One for Me?** In it, she asks all the pertinent questions that young lovers never ask. Why? Their main attraction at an early age centers around sex, more sex and as much sex as possible.

You're smiling! Of course! No one thinks with their brains during courtship! Their brains operate only through their genitals. Most stand guilty of that history!

In the end, couples need to consider a battery of tests, classes and requirements beyond their sexual attraction. They need to address the hard realities of their positive or negative possibilities for a long-term relationship.

Personally, as an elementary school teacher who witnessed many unhappy couples and their kids in my classes—as an ideal I think everyone might be more successful in marriage by waiting until age 25 or older. They need to 'get to know' themselves and their life direction before they 'hook up' with another who possesses no idea where they're headed, either.

Not only that, I suggest waiting for at least three years before they birth a child. With over 50 percent divorce rates, wouldn't it be more prudent and sensible for kids to enjoy two parents in their formative years instead of angry parents and weekend fathers? No wonder we see so much social deviation, drug use and alcohol. People try to eat or drink their pain away. It doesn't work!

In the end, marriage partners better be compatible, best friends, share a lot of activities in common or no matter how rich or good looking they may be—they're screwed. Examples abound: Britney Spears, Michael Jackson, Marie Osmond, Garth Brooks, Elvis Presley, Kim Basinger, Marilyn Monroe, Joe DiMaggio, Judy Garland, Madonna and just about every movie or music star you can name. In their cases, money and fame cannot or did not buy them happiness.

As you can imagine, when it comes to "Meyers-Briggs" compatibility understandings or Enneagram, it's possible that fathers might 'like' one son or daughter over another—depending on matches. The same goes with moms for their children. Natural affinities bond different people in seemingly mysterious ways. But not really! They follow their natural inclinations.

Chapter 15—
Dropping a best friend

"In everyone's life, at some time, our inner fire goes out. It is then burst into flame by an encounter with another human being. We should all be thankful for those people who rekindle the inner spirit."
Albert Schweitzer

Some men carry the emotional makeup of a rattlesnake. They like life by themselves. The environmental writer, Edward Abbey, loved his alone life as a ranger at Arches National Park in Moab, Utah. He loved being a fire-watch sentry where he spent weeks alone. Read his book, **Desert Solitaire,** for a rare taste of life in a desolate place. Brilliant, beautiful, compelling!

Others prefer constant company like you see on those inane football ads where everyone cheers around the TV as they stuff pizza into their mouths. Notice movie stars cannot wait to be seen at the big party. The late Michael Jackson, Angelina Jolie, Madonna, Paris Hilton and many others always work the entertainment headlines.

Still others require only one friend. Many go begging for friends in this highly eclectic world. As you see on TV programs, friends burn friends by lying, cheating and stealing from them. Others betray their friends. It all occurs out there on life's playground.

I met a guy named Trak on a racquetball court. Heck of a competitor! For whatever reason, he didn't give me any cause to like him. Because he worked as a businessman from a very wealthy background, we didn't share much in common. In fact, his money stood head and shoulders out of my league.

And many times, I've found that rich people like to hang with rich people while middle class dudes hang with other middle class dudes. Notwithstanding, poor folks usually hang with poor folk. For certain, drunks hang with drunks at the bar. They speak a language all their own from their alcohol-clouded minds.

Trak suffered the death of his brother from a car accident during his teens. It staggered Trak beyond anyone's imagination. He couldn't quite find his groove nor could he relate to other guys very well.

He seemed needy to me. Nonetheless, we kept playing racquetball with a passion. After two months of playing the 'challenge' court, we finished up a sweaty round by taking showers.

"Hey," Trak said, "you want to grab dinner? My treat!"

"Sure," I said.

It didn't take long before he asked me to go motorcycling with him and his gal. My lady and I agreed to hit some cider stands. Later, we rode bicycles. I found him to be fastidious and proper. His lady presented herself as the New York Marriott type, so I knew I would be in for a rough haul over the long run.

Yet, he pursued a friendship with me for several years. I never really reciprocated, but I did spend time on outings like biking, motorcycling, racquetball and dinners with him and his lady.

Then, one day, I decided to move out of state.

Trak suffered a breakdown pleading, "Are you leaving because of something I did?"

"Hell no, I just need to move back out to Colorado," I said.

"What about our friendship?" he said.

"I don't know," I said. "You could move out to Colorado and we could hit slopes together."

"I can't do that," he said. "My parents live here and they're getting old and need my support."

Truth be told, he tied his own apron-string to his parents by his own hand.

I left without much fanfare. I didn't know it, but years later, another one of my friends who knew Trak, who is a loner, took a bicycle trip with me across the USA. One night by the campfire, Doug said, "You sure broke Trak's heart when you left Michigan."

"What are you talking about?" I said.

"He got busted up pretty bad when you left," Doug said. "I don't think he ever got over it."

"Gees," I said. "I never gave it much thought."

I never gave it much thought because I left the friendship and it didn't mean as much to me as it did to him. Strange how life works! The reason I wrote this book stems from me being on the receiving end of a loss of three of my longest and deepest friends. One of them, a woman, cracked the friendship after 29 years.

Can you change that outcome? Do things breakdown? Do friendships fall apart like an old shoe with a hole in the leather? In the great human drama, can we control friendships or any of what happens to us? I know one thing; you can only give it your best shot, your best integrity and your best emotional investment. If you don't, you may never enjoy a best friend. Sure, you can get your emotional ass kicked, but to live this life without a best friend may be the severest tragedy of all.

No one in this game of life gets out without a few broken bones. If they sit motionless in a rocking chair, they might not get busted up, but they die a brittle death. Same as friendship! If you never shared a dear friendship, sure, you never suffered the hurt from loss—but you never shared the joy of that campfire.

Chapter 16—
Losing your brother as a friend

"Your brother spends your formative years with you, which creates a powerful bond. It can last a lifetime or it can last as long as your last argument."
                                                Unknown

One year apart, my brother Rex and I grew up with an amazing father. He took us camping, traveling and introduced us to every sport possible in our formative years. Both of us, being highly competitive, tried to beat each other in tennis, golf, bowling, baseball, football, basketball, track and handball.

While we tried to win against each other, we accelerated our athletic skills from sheer repetition. While spending time together locked in sports combat, we forged an emotional bond known only to brothers.

In little league baseball, they separated us onto different teams because as catchers and pitchers, no one could beat us if we played on the same team. On opposite teams, we fought like crazy to beat each other. Even that forged our brotherhood into deeper meanings.

In high school, we played on the same teams. Rex became a star linebacker, point guard and gifted baseball pitcher.

We both shared paper routes and both tried to please dad in every way we could.

When our father died during our high school days, we both suffered severe shock and emotional turmoil. A year later, I staggered off to college in a confused state of mind and emotions. However, I regained my bearings and fit pretty well into the university campus atmosphere. A year later, Rex joined me. We commenced to play sports, attend classes and forged our brotherhood into many scrapbook memories.

After college, I married a lady that didn't like Rex, and, we moved to a different city. But the bond remained. However, when I divorced, we again shared adventures with Rex to Alaska on motorcycles, skiing in the Colorado Rockies and wilderness trips.

Then, we traveled to Alaska again on bikes, but suffered an argument. He cast me out of his life for five years. Man! That proved a wrenching experience! I didn't know how to handle it, but, with no choice, I mended as best I could.

Brothers with different styles

It baffled me as to what happened. I suffered a vacancy of the heart that burned into my mind. Was he punishing me? Did he hate me? Was it my fault? It broke me down in many ways as I tried to understand it. But, when it comes to emotions, each human possesses a different 'hard drive'. Also, life writes a different software program onto each person's brain.

Years later, we got back together and shared more wilderness experiences, but again, on another big adventure trip, I found out something that ultimately provided the reasons for our loss of our brotherhood and friendship.

Rex and I had changed into different kinds of human beings. We evolved into conflicting lifestyles. I danced and dined in vegetarian style. Rex smoked, drank and hunted.

While both of us suffered divorces, each of us handled those traumas in different ways. Our emotions suffered a meat grinder effect that spit us out with little resemblance of our former emotional selves.

To this day, we live 8,000 miles apart and never call, write or visit. I suspect we won't see each other for the rest of our lives. He may or may not suffer from it, and, as for me, I have distanced myself from him in order to protect my emotions. Thus, we both handle the situation in our own ways for our own best emotional balance.

We were born brothers and grew into best friendships, but life and conflicting styles pulled us apart or simply wore us away. Years later and miles down the road, I have learned to accept what I cannot change. I have learned to do the best I can while appreciating that everybody paddles their canoes as best they can, too.

If anything like that happens to you, it's best to bless your siblings and wish them well on their journey through life.

Chapter 17— Friends at the later stages of your life

"A friend creates and shares the best times of your life."
Unknown

My friend Don Collins added, perhaps, the greatest wisdom from his 78 years. He offers a perspective of a man with worldwide travel. He remains fully engaged in life more than any man I know. I value his friendship and his counsel.

Don wrote: as one gets older, the memory process becomes not necessarily weaker but rather filled like the hard disc on your computer with so much material that to exhume experiences with their original intensity becomes more difficult. However, perhaps that aging process is then a bit like panning a rushing stream for gold, namely the nuggets you remember are the most important. That process certainly applies at 78 to recollections of old best friends gone. I would suggest that for many of us, there simply can't be one best friend, one that dominates all the others or forces you to exclude several key friends from that exalted list.

Losing Your Best Friend

It is perhaps fashionable and/or comforting to say, for example, "My father was my best friend." Okay, that may indeed be true, but the cumulative process of friendship—its relentlessly serial nature—means that other figures, in my case, my favorite aunt and uncle, really surrogate parents in my life, must stand in strong relief in my memory stream of nuggets.

So what defines a best friend? Is he the one who saved your life in battle? Can she be your mother, the one that led you at critical junctures in the paths of righteousness? Must it be a blood relation? My father always insisted that blood is thicker than prune juice.

Of course any of those could be true, but frankly in the review of nuggets in your strong box of memory, there must be more than one, as you are influenced by a composite of associations and the opinion you might have of a one and only best friend could ironically omit the old maid school teacher who called you on a youthful indiscretion such as cheating on a test in elementary school, thus teaching you a lesson which you carried forever in your later life's dealings. Try that in remembering your nuggets and maybe add one more to that best friend category!

One best friend of mine was my freshman college roommate. He and I grew up in the same home town, a small city in Western Pennsylvania. He was a year ahead of me and was sent off to a college prep school to fatten up for football, while I continued in my high school, an institution not noted for its prep quality.

Somehow we both entered an Ivy League school and by rooming together, I got the benefit of his more mature guidance at a time when I was indeed a naïf among presumed prep school sophisticates, young men who by hailing from the likes of Andover had essentially already covered the freshman year curriculum they were receiving in this liberal arts college. While he went on to great glory as captain of the football team and membership in our college's most elite clubs and groups, I persevered to graduate with reasonable grace, but certainly not with his elevated visibility and status.

But we were always close and enduring friends. He went on to law school after a two year Army stint in Germany, then returned to join his family's law firm in our home town. I went to serve in the US Navy and got a graduate education in management, then an MBA at NYU while working as a credit man at a prestigious NYC bank. Throughout we stayed in touch.

When I moved to work in a city near our home town, then to live as a commuter in my old home town, we resumed that friendship at closer range. Subsequent events took me to the West Coast to live and yet we had bonded as few do.

When I again moved east, we got together regularly, including visits he and his wife made to my city. Suddenly, this straight arrow, tee-totaling man whose life had been lived in the healthiest manner contracted terminal cancer and died suddenly before many of us knew he was ill.

I won't name all the close times we shared together, including our competition at tennis and squash where we had fiercely contested bouts, or the personal anguishes about our sometimes complex family lives or the joys we also savored over what was a 40 plus year friendship.

However, I will tell you that at my bedside is the photo of him and me sitting in my living room smiling together on his last visit to my present city, a memorable evening with our beloved spouses. The warmth of that friendship endures with daily remembrances and joins several relationships in my long life of similar intensity, underlining my thesis that there is always more than one "best friend" in most lives.

Chapter 18—
Losing a friend too soon

"You never know when your best friend will be gone."
Al Wilson

Al Wilson relates this story from his youth with his best friend: Back in the early years of my life, I met someone who was destined to become my best friend. Being a little over three years of age myself, I really wasn't aware of it at that moment. This introduction took place in Conifer, Colorado. He carried the name of Russell.

As time went along we got better acquainted as we played together. Due to our age difference, the friendship ebbed and flowed. I had other, older friends and he had his younger friends. His younger buddies would try to tag along with me and my older buddies. My worst recollection was when his gang was following my gang around the neighborhood. Someone threw a rock at another. A wall of stones volleyed back and forth. Caught up in the battle, I remember taking aim on my friend Russell. I heaved that stone with great accuracy and very poor judgment. It hit him on the head right above his left eye. It knocked him out—lots of blood! Blood all over the place! The battle came to a quick close with great worry of the parental consequences. The penalties were minimal but in my mind the wound went deep. Deep into my conscience! It has stayed with me for years after that stone was thrown.

We built forts, climbed trees, rode bikes, caught butterflies, read comics and collected rocks. Every story about growing up with a friend would not be complete without the things that we shared that the local authorities were never supposed to know about. But they always seemed to find out before the day was completed.

Three friends one fall day decided to harass the busy highway in the neighborhood. Steve, Russell and I began pulling up grass clumps with the balls of dirt clinging to the roots. These dirt clumps made wonderful flinging devices. We would wind up and hurl them onto the road surface from the bank below. Our first few cars came upon our grass clumps with braking and caution.

They maneuvered slowly through our road hazards. Over the next 15 minutes we had tossed some 50-75 clumps. It was exciting for the moment, but our sleds were calling us to the frozen surface of the creek bottom below the highway. It was quiet for about 20 minutes until the state highway patrolman stopped and used his shovel to remove all the debris on the highway above.

We were a little nervous but thought the patrolman would never suspect us in this moment of boyhood fun. So we moved farther away from the highway and became less visible from the open creek bottom. Well, the shoveling noise stopped and the patrolman drove south. We felt a little relieved but turned our attention to whatever the patrolman might do. He might turn onto our road that ran in front of my house. Terror struck our hearts!

We moved farther up the hill and away from the crime scene. Then, without evidence and without provocation, the patrolman slowed down and turned into my driveway. He stopped just short of the gate that blocked him from us. Surely he did not suspect us of anything. He got out of his car, looked up the hill towards us as if he had us on radar all the time. He yelled out, "Boys, would you come down here please." Oh my goodness we thought! What do we do now? Whatever happens I will be okay because my parents are not home and we won't have to tell anybody. So, down the hill we walked to the patrolman like he asked. As we stood facing him, he began by asking us if we knew anything about the dirt clods on the highway. Without hesitation we assured him we knew nothing about them. It must have been some other kids in the neighborhood.

Other conversation ensued and we were feeling relieved that he had not accused us directly. Until he told us that he was coming back to visit all our parents to sort out this matter! Further, we should all go straight home and tell our parents what had happened and that he would be back to talk with them. We looked at each other and thought, sure! Right!

I'm going to tell my parents. No way! As the patrolman drove off, Steve looked toward his house only to point out his mother and two sisters were looking through the picture window observing the whole thing. Reality hit! We were in trouble. If his mother knew, my parents would know. So, we walked home and told our respective parents all about what we had done. The patrolman never returned. He didn't need to. He knew what he was doing and that we would do exactly as he had told us.

The years rolled on. I left the neighborhood for college. We kept up with each other through our parents. A couple of years later, Russell and I met again. We shared stories about our continuing trials with parents, school, girls and life in general.

Out comes a story about deceiving the watchful eye of his parents. A story about faking illness! A brazen escape from the second story window, lowering himself to the ground with a rope and a day skiing with friends! Wow, I could have never gotten away with that. I could only admire and respect such daring bravery.

But the story that set our friendship with the highest love and respect came from an account I will never forget.

It is all about a girlfriend with another older neighbor. Russ told me that the other fellow had told the girlfriend things that would impress her and leave Russell looking like the bad guy. After Russell heard about this, he left his house and drove to the location where the perpetrator of these lies worked. Russell climbed up on the gravel crusher and approached this fellow.

He told this guy to meet him at Russell's home after work. I was at Russell's house when he returned. Russ told me about all the details when this fellow drove into the yard. Russ met him at the front steps. There were words about making someone look bad.

And making up stories to make him look like something he was not. The thing that piqued my interest was Russell telling him he should apologize. I could not hear what this fellow said but he got the lickin' of his life. Without further words, he left with a bloody face in a cloud of dust.

Wow! I had respect for this man now. After all these years sharing the things that we had shared, yes, we shared a bond for life!

Back to college I went to finish my studies. Russell graduated from high school and joined the Navy. I found the love of my life and got married. I invited Russell to be my best man at the wedding. He could not come as he had just been deployed on his first assignment in Naples, Italy. I was disappointed, but knew that we had shared so much in our lives and that we would catch up sometime in the future.

A couple of months later, I traveled with my new wife to visit her family near Washington, DC. On an intermediate stop in Kansas City, I called my aunt, my dad's sister to let her know we were on our way and the time we would arrive. There was silence. She broke the silence telling me to call my dad at home. Something had happened. He would explain. I hung up and called home.

As I listened to the phone ring, I looked out upon the lovely high ceiling of the downtown Kansas City airport terminal building. Through the old glass windows of the phone booth! My gaze was interrupted by thoughts of one of my grandparents passing away.

Losing Your Best Friend

As my dad's saddened voice explained that the grandparents were okay, he explained that Russell had an accident hear Naples in a little VW and had perished.

I sank to the floor in a trembling rage that fell into tears. The visions of our friendship passed before my eyes. All the things we had done together through the years were over in an instant. He was a tender young age of 19 years old and the sharing ended with this tragic accident. The sharing was very deep, as we shared more than this story has let on. We shared life, we shared a house together, a room together. We shared blood and parents and all the things that go with being brothers. Yes, Russell was my brother and my best friend.

Chapter 19—
Do it while you're young

"Some friends arrive for a reason, season or lifetime."
Brian Chalker

Did you ever wonder why a friend would enjoy four years of incredible adventures in college, but quickly make excuses to avoid his youth—while he plunged into the work-world that lasts for the next 40 years? Such a story happened to my brother Howard. He relates it:

The very first time I watched the TV comedy, **The 70s Show**, I booted up my computer to locate my best friend of the 70s, Bob Besselievre. We had lived through the moments depicted on the screen and it was such a hoot to see them recreated.

As I sat down, I stopped, reflected and then realized there was no point. Since we broke up the student house in 1976, I had contacted him 5-6 times with no reciprocation. My last Christmas letter came back "Addressee Unknown."

Sighing heavily and with sadness in my heart, I went to my email and had a normal evening.

Bob and I became suite-mates at Michigan State University in the fall of 1971. His dad had been a high-level executive at Ford and Bob declared he would follow in his dad's footsteps. His dad had recently died of a brain aneurysm and mine had died when I was 13 of a heart attack. We immediately had something in common and we hit it off well.

Bob and I had a lot in common. We hated the war, smoked dope, loved women and studied just enough to pass our courses. We both worked as student cooks in the residence halls. We hung out together for all social events. We even joined another 20 students in 1973 to drive a Ryder truck to DC to protest Nixon's inauguration. I was driving when the Ohio State Trooper pulled me over for defective running lights. I was able to remain calm enough and the trooper never asked to search the truck which would have destroyed 22 lives, as we all had a three day supply of pot. Ah, the wild times!

All good student days come to an end and so it was in March 1976. But before we split up, Bob and I made a solemn pact to tour Europe on motorcycles in the summer of 1977. He would work as the assistant manager of a fancy restaurant for 15 months, live with mom and thus would earn the money. I drove a United Van Lines 18-wheeler that summer moving furniture for families being transferred to other parts of the country.

I shipped my new Honda 750 to Europe and rode it to a family in Germany. Bob and I wrote letters back and forth about the coming 'Easy Rider' summer we would soon share and enjoy. We had both watched the movie by Peter Fonda and Dennis Hopper as they rode their 'Hogs' across America. Free, fun, women and the open road! We were about to step right into our dreams.

I was excited to share the adventure of the road with my best friend and he was excited to see Europe for the first time with someone who was experienced with the road to adventure.

Two months before Bob was to due to depart, the letter arrived. Bob wrote that his career in restaurant management would suffer seriously if he became irresponsible and quit his job to have fun. It would look bad on the resume. Bob wrote of going over some other time and spending a few weeks. And blah, blah, blah! I knew the decision was irrevocable. I wrote back a nice note, saying I understood. I did not know that our relationship was finished.

Bob didn't realize that by not taking the trip with me, he would never take the ride. He passed up 'that' moment in time, and, sadly, he could never get it back again. He never fulfilled that wanderlust of his youth. Over the years, I've listened to many a story by many a guy regretting not having taken 'that' adventure to some great place on the planet.

Nine years later I spent a few hours visiting Bob in Orlando. He had recently quit as the manager of a major hotel, as the stress was killing him. He was a bartender and enjoying it. He had become a husband and father with the attendant responsibilities.

He said he regretted not seizing the moment in 1977. He realized too late that it would have made no difference, whether he quit or not to have that one mega adventure of his life. The ride and memories were not 'in' him and he lamented that decision. Now it would have to wait another 20 years till his kids finished college. We promised to stay in touch but my next two letters went unanswered.

The flood of great memories of **"*The 70s Show*"** probably found many friends reaching out again to a lost buddy, but I realized that it would be useless. The friendship was dead and no phone call would breathe life into it. Too bad! Too sad!

I will never comprehend how two people (outside of a marriage and divorce) can share so much, care so much and then like a light switch, and turn it off. Or maybe the feelings were never as great from him as I believed. Who knows? It is all spilt milk. We only go around once in life. I am not going back to college and do it all over again. I sigh; I shake my head and remember the good years we had together. Memories! That is all there is left.

Why I cared enough to keep contact and he didn't still mystifies me years and miles down the road. What we shared was SO good!

When all of us take our last breath, it won't be about the money, house, fame, fortune or status: for the most fortunate, it's about our friends.

I know one thing, few men understand the importance of friendships. They let slip a precious connection to life, a buddy, shared memories and mutual interests.

The lesson learned: take those adventures in your younger years, because, once you get caught up in the working world and marriage, life carries you away from your youthful wildness and yearning to explore the world. In other words, do it while you're young.

When you do, you will enjoy memories and photo albums that will be treasured more than you realize at the time you shared the adventure with your best friend.

Chapter 20—
Losing a friend
you never met

"I loved John Denver like a brother but I never met him."
A fan

Entertainers like John Denver, Farrah Fawcett, Michael Jackson, Raquel Welch, Willie Nelson, Lucille Ball, Garth Brooks, Nicole Kidman, Elvis Presley, John Wayne, Marilyn Monroe, Ella Fitzgerald, Denzel Washington, Tom Cruise, Paul Newman, Meryl Streep, Clint Eastwood, Julia Roberts, Tiger Woods, Alex Rodriguez, Tom Brady, Clinton Portis, Champ Bailey, Wayne Gretzsky and others become emotional threads in the formation of our lives.

We may be touched by their music, sports or by their heroics in the movies. One thing stands out, they impact us emotionally.

I've seen every one of Clint Eastwood's movies a half dozen times. I even shook hands with Clint, yup, little old me, shook hands with a legend!

John Denver's songs play on my CDs, but more importantly, they play in my heart. I am a country boy! I love Colorado! I love sitting by a campfire with shooting stars dancing across the night sky.

I loved Julia Roberts in "Pretty Woman" and Meryl Streep in "Bridges of Madison County" and "Mama Mia". Remember Marilyn Monroe in "Some Like it Hot"?

We become attached to the icons of our era. Since I've been a dancer all my life, I danced to Elvis Presley, Roy Orbison, James Brown, Michael Jackson and many others. Their songs wrote powerful lines in the chapters of my life book.

When Elvis died, August 16, 1977, I felt blown away. He died at 43! His drug use and early death upset me. How could he die when he enjoyed so much money and fame? He had SO many more songs to sing. It took me a long time to get used to his passing. I finally realized that he suffered more problems than the usual man because fans mobbed him, the paparazzi hounded him, women lavished him, his wife left him and fame overwhelmed him. He took to drugs and overeating. He became isolated and a recluse. He may have died from poor diet and a heart attack, but for the most part, he died of a broken heart.

Look at the drama surrounding Michael Jackson's death! People mourned all over the world. Music and the music makers play a deeply emotional part of our lives.

When big John Wayne died, I couldn't believe it. My heroes shouldn't die. But, he died. So did Jimmy Stewart that you see every Christmas in "It's a Wonderful Life!"

Losing Your Best Friend

Because I had danced so much to John Denver's romantic songs and had lived much of what he wrote about—I felt a tremendous connection to him as a 'friend' even though I never met him. I did see him play at Red Rocks in Morrison, Colorado at a huge outdoor concert. I will never forget his rendition of a "Country Boy" and "The Old Feather Bed" or "Annie" or "Colorado Rocky Mountain High, I've seen it raining fire in the sky...."

Yes, he connected with so many via his music. He touched their hearts. He touched mine, too. Music forms powerful connections in a person's mind and emotions.

Out of the blue, John Denver died in an airplane crash. Previous to that crash, he suffered two DUIs, smashed up two cars and faced two broken marriages. It shows that no one escapes this life without trouble and pain. You would think he enjoyed every privilege of wealth and fame. He could fulfill every dream, but, in the end, he couldn't. They say he ran out of fuel in his plane that crashed, but I think he ran out of purpose, passion and love.

That's what may have killed him. But his death killed a bit of my spirit, too. I felt depressed for several weeks. I still play his songs, but I know he's no longer with us, but he should be. He died in his 50s. Too soon and too many more songs to sing!

Why do so many Americans experience the death of a movie star, sports hero or singer on a personal level?

"People feel it profoundly because celebrities are a part of our day-to-day as a culture," said Liz Wagner, a

Denver, Colorado grief counselor. "It's a concrete loss, but also an ambiguous loss because we hold celebrities as idols or heroes."

Author Leo Braudy said, "We have a symbiotic relationship with celebrities' lives. A little part of our psychic lives die as well when a celebrity dies."

As you can imagine, with conflicting dynamics, such stars as Monroe, James Dean, John F. Kennedy, Elvis and Michael Jackson—continue 'living' decades after their deaths because of their 'conflicted' lives.

Somehow, 'conflict' creates interest. Whereas, someone that leads a normal life proves uninteresting to the media.

Finally, those stars fill a nostalgic aspect of our own lives and once they die, that nostalgic remembrance fades, but we hold on to the memories.

More big singers and movie stars will die during my time on this planet. However, I will celebrate their lives, songs and movies even though they don't know that I consider them my 'friends'.

For each of us average people, enjoy those singers or movie stars because they touch our hearts and minds. We form special 'bonds' with them that affect our lives in positive ways. Makes for a most amazing ride through life!

Chapter 21—
How to lessen your chances of losing a best friend

"Thus nature has no love for solitude, and always leans, as it were, on some support; and the sweetest support is found in the most intimate friendship."
                                                            Ciscero

Have I learned a few lessons during my lifetime? You betcha! Can you take advantage of my mistakes? Darn right you can, if they fit your style or circumstance!

Lesson # 1

If your best friend sports a girlfriend or wife, you're going to meet her at some point. It's a crap shoot whether or not she may like you; if you're the quiet, reserved type and don't present any threat, you may be okay.

If you're the high spirited type, you may want to tone yourself down when meeting her. Sincerely compliment her about something you find attractive. Ask questions.

Listen to her stories. If she doesn't talk much, try to engage your friend to engage her.

Never say anything that she can use against you. Avoid talking about sex or anything intimate. Avoid religion or politics. Don't make any off-handed jokes. Talk to her friends about 'chick flicks' like "Mama Mia" or their latest avocation. Women knit themselves together. Anything you say to one you say to all of them. Saying good things brings unending dividends!

If it's a party, offer to clean up the place and wash the dishes. Women love guys pitching in to clean up.

Be friendly, but keep out of the house for the most part so you won't tread on her territory.

If Ron could take back time, he would have never visited Al's house other than for Thanksgiving or a birthday party. Ron would have made sure he didn't give Al's wife any ammunition to use against him.

If your friend's wife is bossy, or insecure, your best bet is to keep your distance.

As long as you see your friend outside the house and never tread on her territory, you may enjoy years of uninterrupted friendship.

Lesson # 2

If your friend never asks you for advice, never give it no matter how much he's hurting. Some guys are only equipped to work things out for themselves. If he does ask, and you give it, you can expect it to come back and bite you on the fanny one day. Most guys will talk to their women, which makes you the instant enemy.

I found that some of my friends were insecure in themselves so they married insecure women, or angry women, or 'victim' women, or dominant women.

How do I know? Several of my friends married top notch ladies who loved themselves, loved their man and saw me as an asset to their man. I've enjoyed a dozen buddies over the past three decades whose wives welcome me into their lives. Now, that's maturity, balance and self-confidence!

However, no matter how great a friendship you enjoy or how many decades, if she doesn't like you, you're toast as long as your friend stays with her.

Okay, I know, you're an emotional guy that cares about your friend, or, about the girlfriend that he's breaking up with!

She calls you for advice. What do you do? Back your tail-feathers out of that situation as fast as a duck paddling away from a fox! Fly like a Canada goose taking off from a coyote on his rear-end! Run like a deer with a pack of wolves on his tail to the next county! You might say that insanity runs in your family and you possess the worst case of it. Tell her that last time you gave advice, he shot your relatives.

Lesson # 3

How do you get over the pain of losing your best friend?

Write a book! Yes, write a book. Write out your pain. Write out the lessons you learned. Write your diary. Keep writing until you drain all the anger and all the pain from your mind, your spirit and your body.

If it comes back, start writing again. You need to get rid of the dump truck full of pain inside your head. If you can talk it out, then, talk it out. I discovered that when you write it out, it takes 'mental anguish thought waves' out of your head and down onto hard copy.

Otherwise, it's like your head acts like a clothes-dryer. The clothes dry, then cook, then shred and keep revolving in your dryer. Take them out by writing them down. Try it! It works!

Also, you may go to a shrink, life coach or someone trained in loss therapy if talking to a professional works better for you. I know it hurts! Why do you think I wrote this book?

Lesson # 4

After you've mourned your loss, get your butt back into the game of life. Join a ski club, bicycle club, chess club, swim club, bridge club, climbing club or any civic group where guys like you share weekly meetings or events.

You may play checkers, chess, cribbage, bridge or go bowling. Meet up with your type of friend by doing things where your kind of friends hang out.

You're bound to meet another dude that might become your best friend. Or, you might meet several dudes in different areas that like to do the same things you like to do.

Lesson # 5

Yes, you must grieve for as long as it takes. The trick for many men—they beat a dead horse longer than needed.

"Many of us spend our whole lives running from our feelings, with the mistaken belief that we cannot bear the pain. But we have already borne the pain. What we have not done is feel all that we are—beyond that pain." Gibran

Celebrate life every day you wake up. Avoid feeling sorry for yourself. You're on a great adventure afforded a limited number of humans on this planet. You enjoy opportunities extraordinary in the scheme of things.

Employ the "Law of Attraction" and move into the "Quantum Field of Possibilities" within your life by giving off 'good vibrations' that attract people rather than repel them. Speak positively and present a positive attitude. By your actions and words, you thrust into the 'quantum field' amazing energy that responds.

Lesson # 6

Finally, when you meet a guy who might become a friend, but you both entertain different politics or religions—agree to avoid talking about subjects that create discord or tension.

Epilogue

Life flows through each of us as unlimited creative expression. By our energy, zest and smile, we attract others. In fact, we attract life. Imagine this gift, this amazing lifetime filled with experiences! What makes it worthwhile? Friends!

It matters little whether they are cats, dogs, horses, men, women, husbands, wives or your pet fish! Our friends share precious time with us on this marvelous planet. Since we all possess a limited amount of time, it's important to grab for the gusto, the adventure and friends along the way that make it relevant to our beings.

Whether they arrive for a reason, season or lifetime—life offers us a banquet table loaded with food, drink and laughter. Let's treasure our best friends as we toast life!

And, when it's all over, you lived it to the fullest, wore yourself out and laughed the loudest in the company of your best friends—be they one or a dozen!

About the Author

Frosty Wooldridge graduated from Michigan State University. He is an environmentalist, mountain climber, Scuba diver, dancer, skier, writer, speaker and photographer. He has taught at the elementary, high school and college levels. He bicycled 100,000 miles on six continents and six times across the United States. His feature articles have appeared in national and international magazines for 30 years. He has interviewed on NBC, CBS, ABC, CNN, FOX and 150 radio shows. He writes bi-weekly columns for 40 web sites including www.NewsWithViews.com; www.AmericanChronicle.com; www.neighbors.DenverPost.com; www.nationalwriterssyndicate.com. He is the author of *Handbook for Touring Bicyclists; Strike Three! Take Your Base; An Extreme Encounter: Antarctica; Bicycling Around the World: Tire Tracks for your Imagination; Motorcycle Adventure to Alaska: Into the Wind; Bicycling The Continental Divide: Slice of Heaven, Taste of Hell; Immigration's Unarmed Invasion: Deadly Consequences; America on the Brink: The Next Added 100 Million Americans.* He presents a program to conferences and colleges across the USA: "*The Coming Population Crisis in America: and what you can do about it.*" He lives in Louisville, CO   www.frostywooldridge.com

Made in the USA
Middletown, DE
24 September 2021

48994704R00078